CRAFTSMAN HOUSES
THE 1913 CATALOG

By Gustav Stickley

Dover Publications, Inc.
Mineola, New York

Bibliographical Note

This Dover edition, first published in 2009, is a republication of the text and illustrations of the catalog first published by The Craftsman Publishing Company, New York, 1913. The layout has been altered for this edition.

International Standard Book Number
ISBN-13: 978-0-486-47005-4
ISBN-10: 0-486-47005-9

Manufactured in the United States by Courier Corporation
47005901
www.doverpublications.com

AN OUTSIDE POINT OF VIEW UPON
THE CRAFTSMAN MOVEMENT

"A CENTURY or even a half century ago the living room was the joy of the log home or the more pretentious mansion. A big fireplace was the center of attraction and here all the household spent the long evenings in democratic fashion. The big kitchen was the dining room also, and here the old-fashioned range furnished both heat and gustatory splendor for the big family.

"Then the heating stove came and the living room was cut into smaller rooms and floors had to be carpeted and furniture plush-upholstered and windows hung with heavy lambrequins and God's sunlight and pure air very much kept out of the house.

"Then came this man—Gustav Stickley—who longed for the freedom and roominess of other days, who saw that the fuel question and the servant question and the question of health must all be reckoned with in the architecture of the modern home; and so he began to plan homes suited to the lives of the people, as reasonable as could be made for the rearing of families who did not want to live beyond their income.

"He saw that many of the problems of life in the home were the result of thoughtless and inartistic architecture, and that if convenience were linked with beauty, economy with good taste, the home life could be made not only a joy and luxury, but a positive influence in molding public opinion and law.

"Hence we have the outdoor sleeping porch that started the crusade against the white plague; we have the big screened porch where we live most of our summer-time; we have the uncarpeted floors where germs cannot lurk, already a potential influence on laws of sanitation for the crowded city quarters."

Editorial by W. F. Muse in
Mason City Globe Gazette

CRAFTSMAN SERVICE AND HOW TO TAKE ADVANTAGE OF IT

FROM the beginning, one of the chief aims of the Craftsman movement has been to encourage and assist all who are interested in the planning, building and furnishing of simple, economical and permanently comfortable homes. It was with this ideal in mind that Gustav Stickley created Craftsman Furniture, designed Craftsman Houses and published THE CRAFTSMAN Magazine.

Now that the movement has grown and spread—now that men and women all over the country are looking more and more to the Craftsman organization as a source of inspiration and practical help—we feel that the time has come to increase the scope and efficiency of Craftsman Service so that it may be more readily available for a greater number of people.

With this object in view, we have organized, under the head of Craftsman Service for Subscribers, the following departments: Craftsman Architectural Service, Craftsman Real-Estate Service, and Craftsman Landscape and Agricultural Service.

We confine our Service to subscribers not because it is a premium with the subscription, but because we feel that no one who is sincerely in sympathy with the Craftsman movement will want to miss a single copy of the magazine. And so, in writing us, home-builders and others who wish to avail themselves of our Service will of course send in their subscription to THE CRAFTSMAN.

The magazine itself will prove invaluable to everyone who is interested in home-making, civic improvement, agriculture, general education, arts or handicrafts. And the only way in which readers can really get the benefit of our work and experience along these lines is by keeping in close touch with the magazine, and following its presentation of whatever seems progressive and worth while in any vital phase of life and work.

CRAFTSMAN SERVICE

THIS LITTLE SHINGLED BUNGALOW
CONTAINS A LARGE LIVING ROOM,
KITCHEN AND BEDROOM, AND
COULD BE USED FOR EITHER A
SUMMER OR ALL-YEAR HOME.

CRAFTSMAN
BUNGALOW
NO. 54.

"THE CRAFTSMAN IS GIVING TO THE AMERICAN PEOPLE A SANE AND SATISFYING PHILOSOPHY OF LIFE AND ITS FUNDAMENTAL LAWS OF BEAUTY."—*Columbus (O.) Dispatch.*

CRAFTSMAN SERVICE

CRAFTSMAN Service will furnish a reliable source of information for all who are interested in the subjects of which the magazine treats. And the more this Service develops, the more closely shall we be able to coöperate with the thousands of Craftsman subscribers all over the country; their common interests will be cemented, by our organization, into a sort of Craftsman fraternity.

Advice and suggestions will be given without charge whenever possible, on such problems as home-planning and construction, building materials, interior decoration, furnishing and equipment (lighting fixtures, hardware, heating apparatus, etc.), greenhouses, landscape, flower, fruit and vegetable gardens, and other matters pertaining to the home and its surroundings.

The only exception will be in cases where the service required involves the drawing of plans or layouts or work of a similar character. In this event we should naturally have to make a moderate charge, and we should of course advise our correspondent what this would be before we began the work.

All information asked for should be stated as briefly and concisely as possible, and a stamp should be enclosed for reply. When it seems advisable, we will send a blank on which may be filled in whatever information we shall need to enable us to furnish the advice or suggestions desired.

CRAFTSMAN SERVICE

CRAFTSMAN FIELD-STONE
BUNGALOW NO. 55: THE
INTERIOR CONSISTS OF
LIVING ROOM, KITCHEN,
TWO BEDROOMS AND BATH.

"THE CRAFTSMAN IS CERTAINLY ONE OF THE FINEST MAGAZINES I HAVE SEEN, AND
I READ A GOOD MANY OF THEM, AMERICAN, GERMAN AND FRENCH."—*E. P., Brooklyn, N. Y.*

CRAFTSMAN ARCHITECTURAL SERVICE

FOR example, if the subscriber is interested in Craftsman architecture, and wishes our aid in the planning and building of his home, the blank sent him will contain questions regarding the general style of house desired, number of rooms, porches and special features, the nature of the site, the amountthe owner can afford to spend, the kind of materials and labor available in that locality, and other important details.

When the prospective home-builder is interested in some particular Craftsman house he should state its number and advise us whether the plans would be suitable just as they are or whether they would need to be modified to meet local requirements and individual needs. In the latter event, a list should be made of the various changes desired in the materials, exterior construction and interior arrangement. We will then advise what would be the cost for redrawing the plans and preparing specifications accordingly.

As we have designed and published in THE CRAFTSMAN Magazine over 150 different houses of various sizes and descriptions, ranging from log camps and rustic bungalows for woodland sites to one-, two- and three-story houses for country, suburban and city lots, it is very likely that the subscriber may find among our designs one which will suit his needs, either just as it stands or with a few alterations.

In any case, this collection of designs, combined with our practical experience in planning and building Craftsman houses, makes it possible for us to furnish plans and specifications at much lower cost than could be obtained elsewhere. And naturally, if the house is to be built along Craftsman lines, no one but ourselves is qualified to furnish the proper drawings and instructions.

In every instance, it should be remembered, the main object of our Architectural Service is *to enable people to build the kind of homes they want for the lowest possible price.*

CRAFTSMAN ARCHITECTURAL SERVICE

CLAPBOARD AND SHINGLE BUNGALOW, NO. 53: IT CONTAINS LIVING ROOM, KITCHEN, TWO BEDROOMS AND BATHROOM, AS WELL AS AN OPEN-AIR DINING ROOM, AN ILLUSTRATION OF WHICH WILL BE FOUND ON PAGE 39.

CRAFTSMAN REAL-ESTATE AND LANDSCAPE SERVICE

CRAFTSMAN REAL-ESTATE SERVICE

IF our subscriber wishes assistance in the selection of a building site or other property, we will send a blank containing questions regarding the kind of land and amount of acreage desired, the purpose for which it is to be used, the amount that can be invested, the location preferred, etc.

On the other hand, if the subscriber has property to sell, we shall provide a blank on which may be entered full details regarding it, for our files, so that we may refer to the owner any of our subscribers who may be looking for property of that description.

When the subscriber has a farm for sale, we will supply a blank on which may be filled in all the necessary details as to the size, nature and location of the property, the kind of soil and crops, average yield per year, nearest market to dispose of products, source of water-supply, quality of roads, improvements installed or available, mortgage if any, and the price and terms on which the owner will sell.

CRAFTSMAN LANDSCAPE AND AGRICULTURAL SERVICE

IF advice is needed on planting, landscape gardening or agriculture, or if the subscriber wishes us to help in the preparation of a garden layout, the blank sent will contain questions as to the style of the house, the size and shape of the grounds, the nature of the soil, the drainage, water-supply and average rainfall, special landscape and architectural features desired, and the amount to be expended in the outdoor development.

In this, as in every other branch of Craftsman Service, we are planning to make our work so efficient and so helpful to our readers all over the country, that our organization will, in itself, be one of the strongest reasons for subscribing to THE CRAFTSMAN Magazine.

"I HAVE NEVER TAKEN A MAGAZINE THAT I HAVE ENJOYED SO THOROUGHLY. IT IS A GREAT DELIGHT TO THE EYE AS WELL AS A FEAST FOR THE MIND."
—*L. I. B. Wauwatosa, Wis.*

PLANNING A CRAFTSMAN HOME

ENTRANCE TO A CRAFTSMAN FIELD-STONE HOUSE: THE SIMPLE, STURDY DOOR IS IN KEEPING WITH THE RUGGED STONEWORK, AND THE SMALL GLASS PANES ARE BOTH PRACTICAL AND DECORATIVE.

PLANNING A CRAFTSMAN HOME

THE PLANNING OF A TYPICAL CRAFTSMAN HOME

ONE of the interesting and significant things about Craftsman architecture is the fact that the comfort and friendliness for which it has become synonymous are the result of the most practical sort of planning and construction. In fact, they have grown out of our simple arrangement of rooms and sturdy structural features as naturally and inevitably as a flower grows out of the soil.

It may be worth while for those who contemplate the building of new homes or the remodeling of old ones, to note how these qualities have been attained, and what particular features contribute most to the atmosphere of restfulness and charm which is endearing Craftsman houses to the hearts of so many American people.

In the first place, we design our houses as simply, economically and durably as possible, with only such rooms and partitions as seem necessary, with no wasted space, no meaningless ornamentation to catch the dust and add to the housewife's labor.

In laying out our floor plans we try to fill all the family needs for both indoor and outdoor living, with openness enough for the common household life and seclusion enough for individual privacy.

And we endeavor always to make the necessary elements of the construction beautiful as well as useful features of the house, relying for decorative effects upon appropriate design, good proportions, harmonious coloring and the natural interest of the materials used.

As the arrangement of the floor plan must always be of more importance to those who live in it than the appearance of the exterior, we determine first the number, size and location of the various rooms, modifying the plans, of course, wherever necessary, so that the exterior of the building will be pleasing in proportion and outline, as well as suitable for the materials and site.

"JUST A GLANCE THROUGH THE PAGES OF THE CRAFTSMAN MAKES ONE FEEL THAT LIFE IS WORTH LIVING AFTER ALL."
—*Wilmington (Del.) Every Evening.*

9

THE CRAFTSMAN DOOR

THE DOOR

THE kind of door chosen for the entrance will depend of course on the style of the house and the personal preference of the owner. For a typical Craftsman home, where a sturdy, unpretentious construction is used throughout, a door of rather simple design would naturally be most in keeping.

The sketch on page 8, which shows the entrance to one of our field-stone houses, gives an example of the sort of door which seems suitable for that particular place. The lower part is made with wood panels and the upper portion is filled by small square panes of leaded glass which light the room within and at the same time add a decorative note to the exterior.

A glance through the views of houses presented in this book will suggest a number of ways in which the design of the door may be varied to suit different conditions and tastes. Sometimes the door may be of plain wood panels, and where it seems desirable one or two rows of amber glass lights may be set across the top. When the door leads into a passageway or hall where a little more light is needed, such construction is useful as well as decorative, and in bedroom doors these small lights are especially attractive, for the amber-colored opalescent glass permits a soft glow of yellow light to penetrate into the hall and at the same time does not destroy the privacy of the room.

When the door opens from a porch or pergola it is a good plan to make it entirely of glass panels, so that as much light as possible will be admitted to the room; for the roof of the porch naturally darkens the windows beneath it a little, and any arrangement that will overcome this objection is welcome.

A glass door is particularly pleasing where there is a vine-clad pergola or an inviting garden beyond, for it permits a full-length vista from the house and gives to the interior a sense of openness and kinship with the outdoor world. Then, too, a door with glass panes adds to the decorative interest of the wall space both outside and in.

THE CRAFTSMAN VESTIBULE

CORNER OF A CRAFTSMAN INTERIOR, SHOWING THE OPEN ARRANGEMENT OF ROOMS. THE VESTIBULE IS ON THE LEFT AND A GLIMPSE OF THE DINING ROOM IS SEEN THROUGH THE WIDE CENTRAL OPENING BESIDE THE STAIRS.

THE CRAFTSMAN VESTIBULE

Where the construction is very plain and rugged, the simplest kind of door would be one made of three or four upright boards, joined on the inside by battens. This style seems especially suitable for summer bungalows and rustic camps such as those shown later on in this book.

It will be noticed that all the doors shown in our illustrations are single. We have not yet found any advantage in using double doors, for they are more expensive and not so simple as the single ones, and are apt not to fit tightly enough to prevent draft.

THE VESTIBULE

WHETHER or not a vestibule is to be included in the plan will depend on the sort of climate and exposure for which the house is intended, as well as on the preference of the owner. Where the winters are very mild, or where the entrance is sufficiently sheltered by a recess or by the roof of a porch, a vestibule would be unnecessary; and where the porch is to be glassed in during the cold months, so that one would cross the enclosed porch to enter the hall or living room, a vestibule would not only be superfluous but would be actually in the way. This point, therefore, must be kept in mind when the floor plan is being worked out.

In designing Craftsman houses we usually protect the front door by a recess, a porch or pergola, and omit the vestibule; but the arrangement can always be changed a little to include one where it seems desirable. On the other hand, in modifying a plan so as to cut down the cost of construction, the vestibule, if shown, is usually one of the features that can be eliminated without spoiling the arrangement.

Where there is a vestibule, or where coat hangers are provided on either side of the entry, or a coat closet on one side and a seat on the other, it is always a good plan to place small windows on each side of the front door, for besides lighting the space within they will add a little to the friendliness of the entrance.

THE CRAFTSMAN VESTIBULE

PART OF A CRAFTSMAN LIVING ROOM, SHOWING A TYPICAL ARRANGEMENT OF ENTRY AND STAIRCASE:
THE WOODWORK, WHILE PRACTICAL AND SIMPLE, IS FULL OF INTEREST.

"AM RENEWING MY SUBSCRIPTION TO THE CRAFTSMAN—I COULD NOT GET ALONG WITHOUT IT; ESPECIALLY AS WE ARE CONTEMPLATING BUILDING A CRAFTSMAN HOME WITHIN THE YEAR."—*G. W. E., Seattle, Wash.*

THE CRAFTSMAN HALL

THE HALL

ONE of the most notable as well as most delightful points about a Craftsman home is the openness of the hall, for we try always to arrange the plan so that on stepping into the house one has a sense of breadth and light and cheerfulness.

In many cases, where the front door is sheltered by a porch, or where a vestibule is provided, the simplest plan is to enter directly into the living room, as one does in Craftsman Bungalows Nos. 116, 118 and 123, shown on pages 68, 70 and 73, in which a separate entrance hall seemed to us unnecessary.

In other plans it seems best to provide an open hall through which one enters the living room, with a convenient coat closet near and possibly a window-seat, as in the plan of House No. 125 on page 76 or No. 154 on page 101.

Sometimes, when the most convenient place for the entrance is at the side of the house, the door may open into a central hall communicating with the living room, kitchen and stairs—a particularly useful plan when a maid is kept, for it allows access from the kitchen to the stairs and front door without passing through the living room.

In fact, there are many practical and pleasant ways in which the hall can be laid out, varying according to the nature of the house and the owner's wishes; but whatever arrangement is chosen, it almost always seems advisable to leave the hall as open as possible, so that it will enhance rather than destroy the wide spaces of the lower floor. This can be done by suggesting and indicating the divisions between the other rooms instead of using solid partitions, and this method affords a chance for an interesting use of woodwork, such as the post-and-panel construction and grilles shown here in some of the interior views. Screens and portières can always be used in the openings when desired, especially in winter when an atmosphere of warmth and comfort is most welcome; while in the summer, when the utmost airiness and freedom

THE CRAFTSMAN STAIRCASE

are wanted indoors, the openings between the hall and rooms can be left wide.

This open type of hallway naturally reduces the cost of construction by the elimination of unnecessary partitions and doors, and by simplifying the plan helps to lessen the housewife's steps. But perhaps the most important thing of all is the fact that it makes even a small house seem spacious, and allows the whole lower floor plan to be thrown open into practically one big room, thus emphasizing the atmosphere of frank comradeship which is such an inviting attribute of a Craftsman home.

THE STAIRCASE

WE have always felt that a staircase, being one of the most important features of a house, deserves a good deal more care in its arrangement and design than is apt to be be-stowed on it; for, when rightly treated, it is an interesting and beautiful part of the interior. It seems to us pre-eminently the one structural element which offers a legitimate opportunity for a decorative use of woodwork, and so in working out our plans we naturally make the most of it, make it a thing of ornament as well as use, build it where it will be a definite addition to the charm of the rooms.

Just how it is arranged depends of course on the rest of the floor plan, as well as on the owner's fancy. Sometimes it seems best to build it in the open hall, with a coat closet beneath, an inviting seat nearby, and perhaps a pleasant landing lighted by a group of casement windows that look down onto the garden; while a newel-post lamp, such as shown on pages 13, 16, and 23, will be found a decorative as well as useful addition.

In other cases it may be more convenient to have the stairs ascend from the living room;

"THE CRAFTSMAN IS ESPECIALLY INTERESTING TO THE HOMEMAKER WHO CONSIDERS A GARDEN AND A CERTAIN AMOUNT OF OUTDOOR LIFE INDISPENSABLE TO HIS HAPPINESS."—*Alexandria (Minn.) Post-News.*

THE CRAFTSMAN STAIRCASE

THIS ILLUSTRATION SUGGESTS A PRACTICAL WAY OF ARRANGING THE STAIRCASE SO THAT IT WILL BE A FRIENDLY DECORATIVE FEATURE OF THE INTERIOR CONSTRUCTION.

this always simplifies the floor plan and adds to the structural interest of the room.

When the arrangement of the house permits, it is a good thing to provide a half-way landing which may be reached also by a few steps from the kitchen. This gives practically the advantage of back stairs without the additional space and expense of a separate staircase.

In comparatively large houses, where one or two maids will probably be kept, it may be advisable to have two separate staircases, one in the front part of the house and another going up from the kitchen or rear hall. And even in designs where we have shown only the one flight of stairs, or the "semi-backstairs" just referred to, a separate back staircase can generally be included, if the owner finds it necessary, by a rearrangement of the plans.

The views on pages 13 and 16 give an idea of the variety of ways in which the staircase may be built, and show what decorative interest its woodwork may give to the interior.

THE LIVING ROOM

THE most used room, and in many respects the most distinctive one in the house is of course the living room. In a typical Craftsman house it is large and airy, made cheerful by many windows that let in the sunlight and frame green vistas of the garden and landscape beyond. If there can be a glass door opening onto the living porch it will make the interior even more attractive. There may be a built-in window-seat or two, provided with a hinged lid to serve the double purpose of comfort and storage, and possibly with bookshelves near at hand—if the arrangement of walls and partitions happens to afford suitable recesses.

The simpler the furnishings of the living room, the better. To our thinking, the most satisfactory way is to have only such things as are really needed and used, so that the room may be easy to keep in order and the advantage of the wide spaces may not be lost.

THE CRAFTSMAN LIVING ROOM

CORNER OF A CRAFTSMAN LIVING ROOM, SHOWING PANELED WOODWORK ON EACH SIDE OF THE CHIMNEYPIECE.

In selecting the furnishings it is always well to choose sturdy, well made pieces, of such materials and construction as will stand the constant wear and tear of daily use—the kind of things that will grow mellower and more livable as time goes on, adding to their own intrinsic beauty that indefinable quality of individuality and sympathetic charm which human contact and association gives to so many common, inanimate things.

"AM SURPRISED AT QUALITY OF WORKMANSHIP ON BOOK RECEIVED (MORE CRAFTSMAN HOMES.) IT IS REALLY A WORK OF ART."—*A. K., Jefferson Bks., Mo.*

THE FIREPLACE IN A CRAFTSMAN HOME

FIREPLACE CORNER OF LIVING ROOM IN A CRAFTSMAN BUNGALOW, SHOWING FIELD-STONE CHIMNEYPIECE AND GENEROUS USE OF WOODWORK.

"I WAS DELIGHTED WITH 'MORE CRAFTSMAN HOMES'! IT IS ONE OF THE MOST INTERESTING BOOKS WHICH I POSSESS."—*W. A. J., Stanford, Ill.*

THE FIREPLACE IN A CRAFTSMAN HOME

THE FIREPLACE

THE center of interest of the lower floor plan is naturally the fireplace—always the symbol of the home. And as a rule the most suitable place for it is in the living room or in an open hall. Around this primitive nucleus the life of the family instinctively gathers, for the glow of happy comradeship as much as for actual warmth. And so it is natural, in working out the plan, to group around the hearth the various structural features and furnishings, and to emphasize the construction of the chimneypiece itself.

If the plan will lend itself to such an arrangement, the fireplace may be made both cosy and picturesque by the building of a nook, slightly screened from the rest of the room by posts and panels or some other decorative extension of the woodwork, and a ceiling beam across the top. This allows the friendly warmth of the fire and the interest of its immediate surroundings to be enjoyed from the main room, and at the same time gives a feeling of semi-privacy about the hearth itself.

Very often, however, it is not practicable to have a nook, as it would complicate the plan and add too much to the expense, and in this case the best place for the chimneypiece is usually in the center of one of the longest wall spaces of the living room, where there will be room for chairs and settles to be grouped around the hearth, and where it will be easily accessible from the rest of the lower floor.

It is always a good plan, when possible, to build one or more fireside seats, with comfortable pillows and a hinged lid so that wood for the fire may be stored there; and if the wall space permits, convenient bookshelves may be built beside the hearth.

As to the chimneypiece itself, there seems no limit to the variety of design and combination of materials that may be used, and perhaps no other feature of the interior offers more interesting scope for originality of expression.

The selection of material for the chimney piece will depend largely on the kind of room in which it is to be built. In a bedroom or any

THE FIREPLACE IN A CRAFTSMAN HOME

CORNER OF A CRAFTSMAN INTERIOR SHOWING TILED CHIMNEYPIECE WITH BOOKSHELVES AT THE SIDE.

place where the woodwork is rather light and the colors and materials of the furnishings are very dainty, the most appropriate thing for the mantel would be wood or tile of some soft shade that would harmonize with the rest of the room. The illustrations used on pages 21, 23 and 30 suggest the type of fireplace suitable for such surroundings.

On the other hand, in a living room or the like, where the woodwork is apt to be more sturdy and deeper in tone, and the furnishings a heavier nature, brick seems the most natural material to use in the chimneypiece, for its rugged air and more or less coarse texture will be in keeping with the trim and furniture about it.

When an unusually rich color effect is wanted, "Tapestry" brick may be employed, for their rough surface and the wide variety of shades in which they are made afford great decorative possibilities. They may be laid in some simple bond with the natural interest of color and texture heightened by wide joints, or they may be arranged to form mosaic designs which will emphasize the "tapestry" effect. In any case, the shades may be selected according to the color scheme of the room— soft tones of red and terra cotta, darker browns with purple or bluish tinges, lighter buffs and yellows and old ivory.

When ordinary clinker brick are to be employed their plainness of color and texture may be broken by a somewhat ornamental bond and by the use of wide joints which always give interest to the surface. It is well not to have too great contrast between the color of the mortar and that of the brick, otherwise a checkered effect will result which might become tiresome to the eye. The illustrations on pages 11, 18, 56 and 116 suggest a number of different ways in which brick mantels can be built.

Field stone can also be used for the chimneypiece with very good effect in certain places, but before deciding on this material it is always well to consider carefully whether it is quite appropriate for the room. The best plan is to use it only in good-sized living rooms or halls

THE FIREPLACE IN A CRAFTSMAN HOME

GLIMPSE OF THE LIVING ROOM IN A CRAFTSMAN HOUSE, WITH TILED CHIMNEYPIECE AND SIMPLE BUT DECORATIVE TREATMENT OF DOORS, WOODWORK AND WALL SPACES: THE STAIRCASE ON THE LEFT WITH ITS NEWEL-POST LAMP ADDS INTEREST TO THE ROOM.

THE FIREPLACE IN A CRAFTSMAN HOME

where very simple, rugged trim and furnishings are employed throughout; otherwise the field stone will be found too heavy and rough in appearance for the rest of the interior. It is usually most successful in a log building, and in country bungalows and mountain camps where a rustic construction is retained both for the exterior and the rooms within. The foregoing, of course, applies to the uncut, irregular-shaped field stone, for the smooth, cut stone, being more formal in appearance than field stone, is not nearly so appropriate for a typical Craftsman interior.

Examples of field-stone fireplaces are presented on pages 19, 26 and 43, the last being in the wall of an open-air dining room where it is especially in keeping with the sturdy construction of walls, pillars and roof.

The design of the chimneypiece is of course an important matter and will be governed largely by personal taste and the space which the fireplace is to occupy. The size and shape of the fireplace opening may be varied according to conditions, and the arch or top of the opening emphasized by a hood, lintel or a variation in the arrangement of the brick, stone or tile. The beauty as well as the usefulness of the chimneypiece can be increased by a thick shelf of wood, preferably long and deep, with an alcove behind that will serve to hold a vase of flowers, a copper bowl, clock or candlesticks.

Another charming and practical addition to the fireplace nook would be some simple Craftsman bracket lamp of hammered metal placed above a seat, or a hanging light suspended from a ceiling beam—wherever it would give the best reading light.

In connection with the fireplace it is interesting to note how rapidly it is coming back into favor with our modern builders. They are incorporating once more in their plans the open hearth whose presence gave such warmth and cheer to Old-World dwellings and our own Colonial homes. And not only is the fireplace being reinstated in the hearts and homes of the people, but even the scope of its efficiency is being increased.

THE FIREPLACE IN A CRAFTSMAN HOME

THIS ILLUSTRATION SHOWS THE FIREPLACE CORNER OF THE LIVING ROOM IN CRAFTSMAN CEMENT COTTAGE NO. 118, WHICH IS PRESENTED ON PAGE 70: THE CONSTRUCTION OF THE CEMENT AND TILE CHIMNEYPIECE, FIRESIDE SEAT AND STAIRWAY IS PARTICULARLY WORTH NOTING.

THE FIREPLACE IN A CRAFTSMAN HOME

VIEW OF THE INGLENOOK IN CRAFTSMAN BUNGALOW NO. 116, EXTERIOR DRAWING AND PLAN OF WHICH WILL BE FOUND ON PAGES 68-69: THE FIELD-STONE FIREPLACE WITH ITS DEEP ALCOVE, WOOD SHELF AND LINTEL, IS ESPECIALLY SUITABLE FOR A RURAL HOME, AND THE WOODWORK OF SEAT AND WALLS CARRIES OUT THE RUGGED EFFECT.

THE LIBRARY OR DEN

IN houses designed for small families, where no maid is to be kept and only a few simple rooms are required, the owner usually does not care for a library or den, the bookcases being placed in some convenient corner of the living room, beside the fireplace or beneath a window group. But where the plan is on a larger and more expensive scale, and a separate library seems desirable, it may be included in the first floor. As a rule it is most practical to have it open out of the hall or living room, somewhat shut away from the rest of the plan so that it will prove a quiet secluded place for study.

Such a room affords an opportunity for an interesting display of woodwork, especially if the bookcases can be built in around the walls, on each side of a chimneypiece, or in an alcove. And here, of all places in a Craftsman house, one expects to find very simple, solid furniture and fittings, at once dignified and friendly, of such arrangement and coloring as will form a restful and harmonious background for reading and work. The illustration on page 28 shows how compact, serviceable and comfortable a library can be made, and how much structural beauty can be attained by a careful use of woodwork and fitments.

THE CRAFTSMAN LIBRARY

ONE CORNER OF THE LIBRARY IN A CRAFTSMAN HOUSE, SHOWING THE ARRANGEMENT OF BUILT-IN BOOKSHELVES, DESK AND WINDOW SEAT.

THE CRAFTSMAN DINING ROOM

THE DINING ROOM

THE arrangement of the dining room will depend a good deal on the size of the house and the purpose for which it is intended. In a rustic bungalow for a mountain, woodland or seashore site, built for summer use only, or in a small cottage for a family of very plain tastes and moderate means, it usually seems advisable to omit the separate dining room and leave space for a table in one corner of the living room, near the kitchen, for the serving of meals. This simplifies the work, fills all practical purposes, and at the same time adds considerably to the frank and democratic air of the home.

If a certain amount of privacy is desired, this end of the room may be curtained off with portières, or a portable screen may be used, either of which will add to the interest of the furnishings and will indicate a division of the room without destroying that openness which is one of the greatest attractions about a Craftsman house.

When the plan is on a somewhat larger scale the dining room may be a nook or alcove opening out of the living room, with possibly a built-in seat against one wall or in a corner where the dining table is to be placed. This not only makes the nook easier to dust and clean, but it also gives it a rather ingenuous, old-fashioned air that reminds one of the Old-World farmhouses where solid-looking benches and settles were placed beside the well filled board.

Even where the owner prefers to have the dining room a good-sized separate room, it always seems well to leave a wide opening into the living room or hall, so that while portières or screens can be used to close it off for privacy during meals, the floor plan can still be left as open as possible the greater part of the time.

Where a sideboard is placed against an outside wall, a row of small windows may be used very effectively above it, while a still more decorative result may be attained if china cabinets are built in on either side. Much variety is pos-

THE CRAFTSMAN DINING ROOM

sible in both the design and placing of such a group, even though the construction be kept simple, and the exact arrangement will depend as much on the owner's taste as on the size and shape of the room. But it is only wise to use the built-in furnishings where they will fill some suitable wall space or fit into some alcove which the plan happens to afford.

BUILT-IN CHINA CLOSETS ON EITHER SIDE OF THE FIREPLACE IN A LIVING ROOM WHICH IS ALSO USED AS A DINING ROOM: BY A SLIGHT DIFFERENCE IN ARRANGEMENT THE CUPBOARDS ABOVE COULD BE MADE TO SERVE AS BOOKCASES AND THOSE BELOW AS STORAGE PLACES FOR PAPERS, MAGAZINES AND THE LIKE.

THE CRAFTSMAN DINING ROOM

WINDOW EXTENDING THE WHOLE WIDTH OF A DINING ROOM AND INTENDED FOR AN EXPOSURE WHERE THERE IS AN ESPECIALLY FINE VIEW.

THE CRAFTSMAN KITCHEN

THE KITCHEN

WHETHER the various tasks of cooking, washing and housekeeping are to be done by the mistress herself or by a maid, the kitchen should of course be as well equipped and as cheerful as possible. Its size and arrangement will be determined by the nature of the house and the needs of the family.

In a farmhouse the kitchen is generally the most important and most frequently used room in the house—a sort of general workroom and living room, in fact. The meals will probably be eaten there, and the family will sit around the fire on long winter evenings much as they did in the old-fashioned kitchens of New England farms. And so, in designing such a house, one would naturally have the kitchen as big and friendly and well lighted as possible, a convenient, cheerful place for the farmer's wife and help to work in, roomy and comfortable enough for friendly gatherings and for meals.

In a suburban or country house a generous kitchen would also be in keeping, especially if the family wished to have most of the meals out there and so dispense with a dining room; but in houses planned for town or city lots, where a separate dining room is preferred, and where much of the food is bought ready cooked or does not need much preparation, a small kitchen or even a kitchenette will be found most suitable.

In any case, it is always desirable to plan a sheltered porch where many of the kitchen tasks, such as the preparing of vegetables, may be done. This will give the housewife or maid a chance to spend as much time as possible in the open air, and will serve as a link between the house and the vegetable garden, if there is one. When a gas or oil stove is used it might be placed on this porch, which could then be used practically as an outdoor kitchen during the warm months; while in winter it might be boarded or glassed in, if the construction would allow.

THE CRAFTSMAN KITCHEN

ARRANGEMENT OF CUPBOARDS, WORK SHELF AND
WINDOWS IN KITCHEN.

A RECESSED WINDOW SEAT THAT WOULD SERVE FOR ANY ROOM IN THE HOUSE.

THE CRAFTSMAN BEDROOMS

THE PANTRY

IN comparatively large houses where a maid is kept, the owner may wish to provide a regular butler's pantry, with sink, drainboards, dressers and shelves, between the dining room and kitchen, with swing doors between—not only for the sake of convenience of china storage and the serving of meals, but also because it prevents any cooking odors from escaping into the front part of the house. But where the housewife does all her own work—and this is coming to be more and more the case—such a pantry would not only be unnecessary but would increase instead of lessen the labor. In this event the equipment usually found in a butler's pantry can be provided in the kitchen. Examples of both arrangements, in various forms, will be found among the floor plans in this book.

THE BEDROOMS

THE sleeping portion of the house will vary, of course, according to the type of the building. In a bungalow, where all the rooms are on one floor, it is advisable to separate the bedrooms and bathroom from the rest of the floor plan for convenience and privacy. In most cases this may be accomplished by the provision of a small hall opening from the living room and communicating with the bathroom and each of the sleeping chambers. Examples of this kind of plan will be found on pages 68, 73, 74, 78, 80 and 90. The details of the arrangement will of course vary in each case.

In a two-story house the simplest plan is to have the stairs go up to a central hall from which the bedrooms and bathroom open. This hall may be lighted by a window on the landing or possibly by a wide opening into an alcove or sewing room in front, such as shown in House No. 153 on page 104. In planning the bedrooms themselves the need of cross ventilation should be kept in mind, and ample closet room should be provided. Storage space can also be contrived, as a rule, in some corner beneath the slope of the roof, or in the attic.

THE CRAFTSMAN BEDROOMS

In a full two-story house the ceilings are all full height and the rooms are usually rectangular; but where the building is only a story and a half high the rooms are apt to be somewhat irregular in shape. The most natural arrangement upstairs, in the latter case, is to plan a room in each gable, and to build a dormer on one or both sides of the house to give headroom to the rest of the second floor.

The rooms in the dormer are generally broken at the corners, owing to the slope of the roof, and thus a sort of recess is formed, which is rather pleasing, for it adds an air of cosiness and permits greater variety of furnishing. Such a recess gives an opportunity for the use of a deep couch or box seat beneath the dormer window, as suggested in the plan of House No. 78 on page 82.

THE BATHROOM

IN locating the bathroom on the second floor the downstairs plan should be kept in mind, and the room so arranged that the plumbing may be carried down concealed in a partition or built-up post—not in an outside wall, for then the pipes would be liable to freeze.

In comparatively small houses where only one bathroom seems necessary, it should of course be accessible from a common hall; but in larger plans it may be desirable to provide an additional bath which may be used as part of a private suite, with bedroom or sleeping balcony, as shown in the plans on pages 89 and 104. When a maid is to be kept a lavatory may be placed downstairs leading out of her room, as in the plans on pages 78 and 90, or an extra bathroom may be included in the attic, as indicated in the plan on page 104.

BUILT-IN FITTINGS

WHILE built-in fittings may add considerably to the comfort and friendliness of a house, there are several points which should be carefully considered before the owner decides to include them in the plans.

CRAFTSMAN BUILT-IN FITTINGS AND WOODWORK

Not only will the fittings add to the cost of construction, but they will require the work of a skilled carpenter—which is sometimes difficult to get. We do not advocate built-in fittings except where the rooms are essentially suited to them—where there is an alcove or recess, or a wall space which they can entirely fill; in other words, where they will be really "fitments" in the sense in which the word is used in England. In such cases the built-in fixtures become a permanent, integral part of the interior construction, and by filling up the recesses or extending across the end of a room they lessen proportionately the floor space and corners to be cleaned.

The exact design of the built-in features will naturally be governed by individual conditions and the owner's fancy and purse, but in a typical Craftsman interior it is always best to keep the construction rather plain, relying on the practical lines and proportions of each piece and the natural interest of the materials to bring about a decorative result. The vari-ations of tone and grain in the wood itself, mellowed and emphasized by a Craftsman stain, and the warm glint of light and color in the hammered copper, brass or iron trim—all these things, while part of a practical construction, will help to make the interior more homelike and beautiful.

SUGGESTION FOR CHIMNEYPIECE IN A SIMPLE BEDROOM.

CRAFTSMAN BUILT-IN FITTINGS AND WOODWORK

THE WOODWORK

THE question of interior trim and finish is one of great interest to the Craftsman home-builder, for so much of the beauty and interest of a room depends on the woodwork.

First the kind of wood should be considered. For the hall, living room and dining room we find that the most suitable woods are oak or chestnut, cypress, ash or elm, as their comparatively coarse texture and definite grain give them a look of rugged frankness that is extremely attractive and satisfying.

Upstairs, where privacy rather than openness is the characteristic of the plan, and where the hangings and decorations are more delicate in both material and coloring than those below, the woods most in keeping are those having a finer and less pronounced grain and a smoother surface. Maple, beech, birch and red gum are among the kinds most appropriate here.

As to the staining and finishing of the wood—we feel always that the most pleasing effects are obtained when the natural interest of grain and texture is retained, and enhanced by deepening the color and at the same time protecting the surface with a soft, mellow finish—choosing preferably some shade of brown, brownish green or gray.

No matter what kind of wood or what color scheme is selected, if the owner wishes to have a typical Craftsman interior he will naturally wish to finish his woodwork along the lines just suggested, using the Craftsman Lustre described on the inside back cover of this book.

PORCHES, SUN ROOMS AND BALCONIES

PEOPLE are coming to believe more and more in the wholesomeness of outdoor living, and they want their houses planned with sheltered porches, pergolas and balconies

CRAFTSMAN PORCHES, SUN ROOMS AND BALCONIES

so that they may work and play, rest and eat, and in many cases sleep also in the open air. Provision for these needs is one of the chief characteristics of a Craftsman house, as a glance through the plans in this book will show.

Just how such open-air accommodation is to be arranged will depend on such factors as the climate in which the house is to be built, the size and cost of the building, the arrangement of rooms and exterior, and the preferences of the family.

Usually a roomy porch can be provided at the front or side of the house, either sheltered by the projecting roof as in the plans on pages 66, 68 and 74, or recessed as shown on pages 73, 76, 78, 86 and 95. This protects the entrance, provides a pleasant place for outdoor living during the summer, and when the construction and exposure are suitable, the space may be glassed in for the winter to form a sun room. In the bungalow plan on page 90 an interior court is shown which suggests in what a variety of ways a sheltered outdoor

SHELTERED ENTRANCE PORCH OF FIELD STONE AND RUSTIC.

CRAFTSMAN PORCHES, SUN ROOMS AND BALCONIES

SUGGESTION FOR RECESSED OPEN-AIR DINING ROOM IN CRAFTSMAN COUNTRY BUNGALOW NO. 53. (SEE PAGE 6).

"THERE IS NOTHING SENSATIONAL ABOUT THE CRAFTSMAN. IT IS ALWAYS WORTH READING."—*Toledo Blade.*

space may be provided. Sometimes a separate dining porch may be arranged opening from the dining room and kitchen, and it is always well to have a kitchen porch for the pleasure and convenience of housewife or maid.

Where the porch projects from the house as shown on page 105, and there is danger of darkening the rooms within, it is a good plan to have a solid roof over the entrance only, and a pergola roof over the rest of the porch.

In planning the sleeping balcony the most convenient way, as a rule, is to have it open from one or more of the bedrooms, and to build it so that it is somewhat sheltered by the roof or sides of the house. Additional protection can of course be given by an awning, if desired. Where there is a dormer a sunken balcony may be built, as in the house illustrated on page 85, and in a construction like that shown on pages 88 or 92 a balcony may be provided under the roof above the recessed porch.

THE WINDOWS

AN important feature of the house is the windows, for they may make or mar the beauty of a room or outside wall. One often finds, on analyzing an unsatisfactory house, that its lack of charm is due to the windows, which, because carelessly arranged, make the house look ordinary. On the other hand, if the windows are well placed and well proportioned with relation to the wall spaces and lines of the building, they may give the place a delightful touch of both architectural and human interest, for they seem to hold more poetry and symbolism than any other part of the building, and merit truly their title—"eyes of the house." In determining the size and location of the windows, therefore, they must be considered from both the interior and exterior point of view. Lighting, ventilation, exposure and views must all be taken into account, and the handling of both inside and outside wall spaces studied. When there is more than one window in the side of a room it is almost best

THE CRAFTSMAN EXTERIOR

to group the windows instead of placing them separately. This gives a wider view, breaks up the wall less, and by focusing the structural interest results in a more decorative effect.

The naturally picturesque quality of a window is generally enhanced by the use of small panes, though where one wishes to take advantage of a pleasant outlook it may be best to use a large pane. In this case a good way is to use a large picture pane in the center with a transom above and small-paned windows on each side, as suggested in the illustrations on pages 87, 99 and 100.

Whether casement or double-hung windows are to be used is another point for the owner to decide; but the casements always add to the friendliness of the house, give it a more rural air and seem especially in keeping with cottage and bungalow construction.

"THE ILLUSTRATIONS IN THE CRAFTS-MAN ARE OF THE HIGHEST ORDER AS USUAL. NO MATTER WHAT THEY ARE, WHETHER FIGURE, NATURE, LANDSCAPE, HOUSE PLANS, THEY ARE AMONG THE BEST OF THEIR KIND."—*Buffalo News.*

THE EXTERIOR

IN a Craftsman house the exterior is the natural outcome of the interior arrangement, guided by the requirements of good construction, proportion and line. Whenever the size of the lot will permit, it seems best to keep the proportions of the house rather long and low, giving a bungalow effect, as this is apt to be more homelike than a higher building.

Naturally, one way to help bring about this result is to set the house as low as possible on the ground, and this, it will be noticed, is one characteristic of our designs. Sometimes it is necessary, however, on account of the cellar lighting, to build the foundation up several feet above the ground. As this makes an unpleasing line around the base of the first story and gives the house the appearance of being cut off from the ground, the best way is to plant shrubs—barberry or evergreens, for instance—near the foundation so that the objectionable line will be concealed or at least partially broken up, and the walls linked to the surrounding garden.

41

THE CRAFTSMAN EXTERIOR

There are many other factors which will help to give the building a low, bungalow air—a long roof with comparatively shallow slope and wide overhanging eaves, long porches and broad groups of windows. Where there are rooms on the second floor a low roof line may be retained by making the house a story and a half high instead of two full stories, and dormers may be provided, varying in construction according to the number and size of the bedrooms and exterior effect desired. The houses on pages 83, 85, 94, 96, 97, 99, 103 and 107 suggest various simple and satisfactory dormer constructions.

The materials of which the house is built will naturally be governed by local conditions and prices, the style of the building, the owner's preference and the amount he can afford to spend. Practically all Craftsman houses can be built of other materials than those in which they are shown, and the plans and specifications adapted accordingly.

For the foundation the most appropriate thing, to our mind, is field stone or quarried stone when these can be easily obtained. Their irregular shape, texture and color make them especially suitable for suburban or country dwellings. We can see no advantage in using cut stone, which being more formal and regular has none of the picturesqueness of the uncut variety. Next in interest comes clinker brick, which seems preferable as a rule to concrete on account of its warm color and the irregular surface afforded by the joints.

The walls, of course, may be of stone, brick, concrete, stucco on brick or metal lath, logs, slabs, clapboards or shingles, or a combination of one or more of these materials, of which various examples will be found among the illustrations here. Sturdiness of construction may be emphasized and interest added to the exterior by the use of heavy beams extending across a gable or supporting the roof of a porch, as shown in the houses on pages 72, 79 and 91.

As to the roof—slate, shingles or composition shingles can be used if the slope is sufficient, while for comparatively flat roofs the

THE CRAFTSMAN EXTERIOR

Fireplace in Open Air Dining Room

"THANK YOU FOR THE BLUE PRINTS OF CONCRETE COTTAGE NO. 133, ALSO FOR THE BOOK 'MORE CRAFTSMAN HOMES.' THE BLUE PRINTS ARE VERY COMPLETE. I SHALL BUILD THIS SUMMER FROM THEM."—*O. S. J., Paris, Ill.*

best thing will be a sheet roofing, such as Ruberoid, the plain surface of which may be broken by battens over the joins.

Either brick or cement may be used for the chimney, or if it is carried up against an outside wall the owner may prefer to build it of field stone. A combination of stone and brick was used in Craftsman House No. 78 with rather pleasing result, as shown on page 83.

The pillars of the porch may be of brick, stone, concrete, or wood—whichever seems to harmonize best with the building. For rustic bungalows and camps the most appropriate thing would be logs, either hewn or left round. Cement, brick or tile will prove most durable for the porch floor.

Whatever the construction of the house, the owner will find it wise to plan and build as simply, durably and economically as possible, and to let the decorative quality of the exterior grow out of the interest of the materials and the design and proportions of the various structural features. A little study of the houses shown in this book will illustrate our

PERGOLA OF COBBLESTONES AND RUSTIC, WITH WISTARIA VINES.

point. The dimensions of the building, the angles of the roof, the grouping of doors and windows, dormers and chimneys, porches and pergolas—these are the factors on which we rely for any beauty our houses may achieve. The use of vines against porch, pergola and trellis, flower boxes between porch posts, at the windows or along a balcony parapet will make the exterior very friendly and inviting, and shrubs, vines and flowers planted at the base of the walls will help to link the building still more closely to the garden.

This fact should be borne in mind especially when the house is first completed; for, like every freshly erected dwelling, it will be sure to have an air of newness, no matter how harmonious materials and colors may be.

A few plants and shrubs against the foundation, some lattice-work up which vines may be coaxed to climb, can be added without much expense. These little garden touches will help to soften any severity of line or surface, making one forget the newness of the place by lending it that air of mellowness which every passing season will deepen.

And as the years go by, if the house is well and wisely built, time and weathering will only enhance its beauty, bringing it still closer to the original ideal—a true Craftsman home.

PLANNING AN INFORMAL GARDEN

WITHIN the last few years the reaction from the hothouse civilization of the city to the more wholesome simplicity of country life has turned the people's thoughts once more to garden-making, and most of them are wondering how they ever managed to do without one so long.

Indeed, this human need of a garden is something on which one can hardly lay too much stress. We need it physically, for the relaxation it affords our bodies and the opportunity it gives for healthy outdoor work and play. We need it spiritually, for the beauty it brings our eyes and the peace it lays upon our souls.

We need it architecturally because it is the natural and appropriate way to link a house to its environment, to bring it into harmony with the landscape by connecting the craftsmanship of man with the work of Nature. But most of all we need it because in practically

THE CRAFTSMAN GARDEN

all of us there is a deep, instinctive longing to possess a little corner of that green Eden from which our modern and materialistic ways of living have made us exiles.

And so most people today who are considering the making of a garden, want it to be primarily *an open-air living place*—a sort of outdoor extension of the indoor home, where they can work and play, read and rest among flowerbeds, lawns and shrubberies, or under the shade of trees and vines which they themselves have helped to lay out, plant and care for. And probably in addition to this they want the garden to furnish them with as many fruits and vegetables as they have space and time to cultivate.

If the owner is fortunate enough to possess a practical knowledge of gardening, so much the better; he will have the pleasure of working out his own problems of arrangement and planting, and will be able to express his own ideas in Nature's language without outside aid.

But those who have more enthusiasm than skill at their command—and there are many of them—need the guidance of an experienced worker to help them put their ideals into tangible form. And it is for such as these that we have organized this branch of

"THE CRAFTSMAN IS A BEAUTIFUL PUBLICATION. IT IS A PITY THAT ALL MAGAZINES CANNOT BE SO EXQUISITELY PUT TOGETHER. A FEW CENTS MORE ON THE COPY WOULD DO IT. I DON'T KNOW WHY ONE BEGRUDGES A DIME MORE FOR A MAGAZINE— AND ORDERS AN EXTRA ENTREE AT THE RESTAURANT FOR TWENTY-FIVE CENTS WITHOUT A QUALM."—*Quoted by C. H. S., California.*

THE CRAFTSMAN GARDEN

Craftsman Service—the Landscape and Agricultural Department.

Our aim here, as in our architecture, is to suggest and advise rather than to dictate; to help our subscribers carry out their individual ideas—not to prescribe our own; in short, to help them make gardens that will be *theirs* in the truest sense of the word, an embodiment of their own wishes, an achievement of their own imagination, work and love.

In order that subscribers may understand clearly our point of view about garden-planning, it may be well to consider briefly some of the most essential points about the layout and planting.

SUGGESTION FOR A RUSTIC GATEWAY.

"I RECEIVED THE BOOK 'MORE CRAFTSMAN HOMES,' AND I FIND IT DIFFICULT TO EXPRESS MY DELIGHT WITH SAME, AS WITH YOUR MAGAZINE. I EXPECT TO BUILD A SMALL FIVE-ROOM HOUSE THIS SUMMER, AND AS IT WILL BE DONE ON A MODEST BASIS, I SHOULD BE GLAD TO RECEIVE ANY SUGGESTIONS YOU HAVE TO OFFER FOR A SUITABLE HOUSE TO BE BUILT ON A 50 FT. LOT, OR ANY SUGGESTIONS YOU COULD GIVE FOR FURNISHING SAME, AS I INTEND TO USE THE CRAFTSMAN FURNISHING THROUGHOUT,"—*F. M., Youngstown, O.*

THE CRAFTSMAN GARDEN

GENERALLY speaking, there are two kinds of gardens—formal and naturalistic. The first is usually most appropriate for large landscape spaces where more or less geometric effects are desired, or in an Italian garden where classic architectural features are introduced.

While very interesting and artistic results can be attained along these lines, the limitation of its arrangement, the expert services required for its making, and the expense which its layout and maintenance generally entail, make a formal garden unsuitable for the needs of most American homes.

On the other hand, a naturalistic or informal garden is apt to be much less expensive, better adapted to small spaces, and more in harmony with our somewhat primitive landscape and the simpler forms which modern architecture is assuming. But perhaps the greatest point in its favor is the fact that the owner can take such a personal, intimate part in its development, making its planning and care a constant expression of individual taste and interest.

Not only is an informal garden a most friendly, companionable background for the simple outdoor life of a family, and a source of comfort and inspiration to those who frequent it, but it may also be a very definite factor in beautifying the community.

For a typical Craftsman home, this sort of garden is especially in keeping—in fact, a formal garden would be quite out of place with such simple, unpretentious houses as those we design. Of course, one can always introduce a few little formal touches, such as a potted shrub on each side of the porch steps, a clipped hedge or bush beside the garden entrance, or some other slightly conventionalized feature that will give a feeling of symmetry to the grounds. But, on the whole, the freer range one gives to Nature's own delightful vagaries of planting and growth, and the less one imposes on them man-made boundaries and restrictions, the more picturesque and inviting the place will be.

In other words, the true Craftsman garden, like the Craftsman home, will be the outcome

THE CRAFTSMAN GARDEN

TRELLIS GATEWAY.

of working along simple but careful lines. And the owner, if he wishes to keep as close as possible to natural beauty, will let the peculiarities of the site, the formation of the soil and the kind of local vegetation suggest the most appropriate plants and the best way to use them.

He will try to take advantage of each irregularity, and work *with* Nature, coaxing, guiding and bending her to the result desired, rather than trying to force her to fit some rigid, predetermined scheme. In this way he will bring into his garden an atmosphere of naïve restfulness and charm, so that it will grow more winsome and lovable with each passing season.

"AM COMPLETING A HOUSE WHICH WE MOVE INTO EARLY IN JUNE, SO PLEASE SEND ME YOUR NEW BOOK 'MORE CRAFTSMAN HOMES' AT THE EARLIEST POSSIBLE DATE. HAVE ADOPTED MANY IDEAS FROM THE ONE I NOW POSSESS."—*W. L. T., Pendleton, Ore.*

THE CRAFTSMAN GARDEN

IN determining the layout of a garden, one of the first things to be considered is the style of the house. When possible, it is a good thing to plan the house and grounds together. But whether this can be done or whether the garden is planned after the house is already built, it is well to keep in mind the close relation between the two, arranging the flower, fruit and vegetable gardens, the paths and lawns; as conveniently as possible, planning pleasant vistas from windows and porches, and placing the summerhouse, rustic seats or other outdoor structures where they will either be secluded from the house or will view it from the most attractive angle.

In planning these architectural features, the natural irregularities of the grounds will usually suggest the most appropriate arrangement. For instance, a little knoll at one end of the lot will be just the place for a rustic arbor with seats and table where one can take tea under the shade of a grape or wistaria vine. A little brook or a dip in the land will suggest a bridge of stone, wood or whatever other

SUGGESTION FOR A RUSTIC GATEWAY AND SEAT.

"I CERTAINLY MUST CONGRATULATE YOU ON THE SPLENDID MAGAZINE. THE FEBRUARY NUMBER, WHICH CONTAINS SEVERAL VERY INTERESTING ARTICLES ESPECIALLY DEALING WITH ENGLISH AND GERMAN MODEL VILLAGES, IS PARTICULARLY PLEASING; AND HAS BEEN VERY MUCH APPRECIATED BY THE MEMBERS OF THE CIVIC COMMITTEE ON A SIMILAR PROJECT CONNECTED WITH THIS CITY."—*P. H. M., Toronto, Canada.*

material seems most in keeping with the house and formation of the land.

A pool or a suitable hollow may form the nucleus for a natural or artificial water garden, while a steep or gentle slope may be utilized for a flight of steps leading up to a summer-house or seat, or perhaps simply to an airy open space.

An old stump may be partially concealed by vines or nasturtiums; a few rocks may invite one to bring in some rich loamy earth and ferns from the nearby woods and start a little fernery; a spreading tree may offer shade for a circular seat around the trunk, and a clump of bushes may serve as the beginning of a shrubbery, or, transplanted, may hide the foundation line of the house or screen a shed or stable from view.

In fact, the more variations the site affords, the greater chance there will be for original and picturesque development.

Much of the charm of the garden will depend on the layout of the paths. If the ground is uneven it is best to have them follow the "lines of least resistance," and usually the more winding they are the more interesting and natural the garden will seem.

Sometimes one can plan a path so that the trees or bushes at one end of it will frame a vista of the hills or woods beyond; sometimes, by a quick turn or a break in trees or shrubbery, an unexpected glimpse of house, landscape or bright flower-beds can be provided. Or an arch, built over the pathway, may frame a specially attractive view beyond and serve at the same time as a support for some flowering vine.

As to the material of which the path is made—this will depend largely on the soil and the style and materials of the house. Gravel, cinders, cement, or even cement and gravel may be used, or brick (laid preferably in some decorative way). The latter always adds a welcome note of warmth and color to the garden, and if brick is used in the house, the path forms a definite architectural link between home and garden.

The boundary lines are equally important. They may be merely indicated by low walls, fences or hedges so that the garden is only slightly screened from its neighbors and its beauty seen from the street; or it may be enclosed for greater privacy by comparatively high walls and hedges that will give a delightful sense of cosiness within and make the garden even more like an "outdoor living room."

Brick, field stone or cement may be used for the walls, and very interesting effects may be attained by a combination of two or more materials—as suggested in the illustration on page 92, where the wall is of stone, the coping of cement and the entrance pillars of brick.

AS to the kind of trees and plants selected for the garden—these will depend on the nature of climate and soil, the owner's preferences and the amount he can afford to spend. In our Northern States it is a good plan, when choosing the trees and shrubs, to include a few evergreens. Then, when winter robs the rest of the garden of its leaves and blossoms, there will still be patches of rich dark green foliage to give a touch of color and friendliness.

If one is planting for the future, good shade trees to select are pin oak, red and scarlet oak, hard maple, white and green ash, and American linden. Norway maples, locusts, poplars and catalpas grow rapidly, while tulip trees are slower to mature. Dogwood will of course add to the beauty of the garden by its white blossoms.

Among the shrubs most suitable for hedges are the California privet, osage orange, Rose of Sharon for a flowering hedge, and barberry for brilliant coloring. Beautiful shrubs for separate planting are the Japanese quince or fire bush, forsythias, weigelias, snowballs, lilacs, strawberry shrub, deutzias, spireas, hydrangeas, viburnums and magnolias.

The hardiest and most graceful vines are Virginia creeper, honeysuckle, wistaria, Boston and Japan ivy, matrimony vine, Dutchman's pipe, Clematis paniculata, and Akebia quinata —the latter a little known but lovely vine bearing clusters of wine-colored blossoms.

The hardiest flowers and those which require the least attention are of course perennials, such as irises, columbines, sweet-williams, garden pinks, forget-me-nots, Oriental poppies, butterfly weed, blanket flowers, perennial asters, hollyhocks, coreopses, lobelias, larkspurs, phlox, hardy chrysanthemums.

Among the popular annuals are sweet peas, nasturtiums, pansies, ragged sailors, poppies, Shirley poppies, sweet alyssum, ageratum and mignonette.

Fruits that can be easily grown are the currants—red, white and black—strawberries, raspberries, blackberries, gooseberries, plums, peaches, cherries, apples and pears. While for a vegetable garden one would probably want lettuce, radishes, peas, beans, cabbages, cauliflowers, Brussels sprouts, celery, asparagus, the many varieties of tomatoes, melons, pumpkins and squash, and Swiss chard, the stalks of which can be used like asparagus and the leaves like lettuce. Wherever possible one should provide for a rotation of crops.

One more point must be mentioned in regard to the planting of the flower garden—namely, the color scheme. No definite rule for this can be given; it must be worked out in each particular case. But one should remember that the better the color harmony, the more closely will the home be linked to its surroundings, and the more restful and satisfying the garden will be.

THE CRAFTSMAN GARDEN

A CEMENT AND RUSTIC PERGOLA THAT WOULD FORM A PLEASANT LINK BETWEEN HOUSE AND GARDEN.

THE CRAFTSMAN FIREPLACE

THE CRAFTSMAN FIREPLACE: A COMPLETE HEATING AND VENTILATING SYSTEM

THE Craftsman Fireplace embodies a complete system of both heating and ventilating, combining the efficiency of a furnace with the comfort and pleasure of an open fire, and, unlike the ordinary furnace, it can be installed in a main room of the house, thus obviating the need of a cellar and consequent waste of heat.

By this system, fresh air is constantly being drawn into the metal heater (concealed in the chimneypiece), warmed and circulated throughout the house.

The room in which the fireplace is located is heated both by the direct radiation of the fire and by the circulation of air from registers in the warm-air chamber in the chimneypiece. Rooms on the same floor, immediately behind or at the side of the chimneypiece (that is, abutting on it) are heated from registers direct (without pipes); and rooms directly over the warm-air chamber are also heated by direct registers. Rooms more distant from the fireplace are reached by warm-air pipes.

By means of the down draft, the greatest possible amount of heat is utilized instead of being lost up the chimney. There can be no back drafts to force smoke and ashes into the room, and sparks cannot escape through the flue to the roof.

The walls of the smoke passages, being vertical, have no ledges where soot or dust could collect, and the soot which falls to the bottom of the smoke chamber can be easily removed through a clean-out door in the back of the fireplace opening.

One Craftsman fireplace will heat five or six rooms, if they are not too far from it, using from seven to ten tons of coal per year in a climate like that of our Central States. The exact amount of fuel depends largely upon the exposure, number and size of the windows, the construction of the house and the care used in running the fireplace.

Coal, coke or wood may be used in a Craftsman fireplace with equal satisfaction. Coal or

THE CRAFTSMAN FIREPLACE

CRAFTSMAN FIREPLACE OF TAPESTRY BRICK, WITH OPEN HEARTH AND
ANDIRONS FOR BURNING WOOD.

THE CRAFTSMAN FIREPLACE

CRAFTSMAN FIREPLACE OF STONE, IN THE HOME OF MR. E. P. SCHEIBE, CAMBRIDGE, MASS.

THE CRAFTSMAN FIREPLACE

coke will furnish a more even heat both day and night than wood; but, because of the slow combustion, due to the down draft, wood will make a good fire from a standpoint of both economy and attention.

The fireplace can be installed either in a new house or in one already built. In the latter case it is necessary to rebuild the chimneypiece to conform to certain inside measurements shown in Figure 3. Otherwise there are no limitations to the design or materials of the chimneypiece.

The cost of the masonry complete with chimney is less than that for the usual fireplace of equal size. For a brick fireplace, about 3,000 brick are required where there is a cellar and the chimney is carried up two stories. At a cost of $10.00 per thousand for brick and an equal sum per thousand for sand, cement and labor, the entire cost of brickwork, including $5.00 for flue lining, would be about $65.00. In a one-story bungalow, with no cellar, it would of course be less.

Common hard-burned brick has been used as a basis for the above figures. Where the owner desires to build the fireplace of concrete, stone, tile or "Tapestry" brick the additional cost will naturally depend on the material selected. Hard-burned brick, at the above cost, if laid up with a wide mortar joint, will make a beautiful fireplace.

The price of the heater complete is $180.00, freight paid, and $300.00 for two when ordered for the same house. This includes the welded iron body, shaking grates (when coal or coke is to be burned), screen, door in ash pit, draft door, registers, sheet metal for ceiling of warm-air chamber, and all irons necessary for carrying brickwork—everything, in fact, except pipes and masonry. If wood only is to be burned, no ash pit is needed and andirons are sent instead of shaking grates.

As shown in Figures 1, 2 and 3, the body of the heater is made of large sheets of non-rusting ingot iron. This is welded together by special welding machinery into one piece

58

THE CRAFTSMAN FIREPLACE

CRAFTSMAN FIREPLACE OF BRICK, IN THE HOME OF MR. D. H. HANCOCK, LARCHMONT, N. Y.

of continuous metal, making leakage of gas, smoke or dust an impossibility. The heater is six feet high, four feet wide, and weighs complete with grates and other iron parts needed in the construction about 1,000 pounds.

Figure 1, which is a vertical section through the fireplace, shows the grates in place for burning coal. The ashes sift through the grates and fall into the ash pit. This arrangement also prevents dust from the ashes escaping into the room.

If preferred, the ash pit can be omitted, and a removable ash pan placed under the grates. The heater is set on the level of the rough floor, and the installation consists in building a brick wall around it. This wall, carried up to the ceiling and roofed over, forms the warm-air chamber. Above this construction only the chimney is required.

In one leg of the chimneypiece is set a metal smoke flue, shown by dotted lines in Figure 3, which is connected with the body of the heater. Above this a tile flue is used. The metal flue starts at the bottom of the smoke outlet on the heater shown in Figure 4, leav-

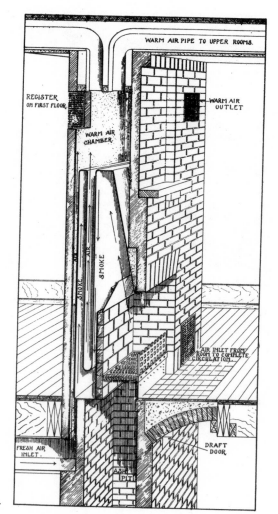

FIG. 1: VERTICAL SECTIONAL PERSPECTIVE OF CRAFTSMAN FIREPLACE.

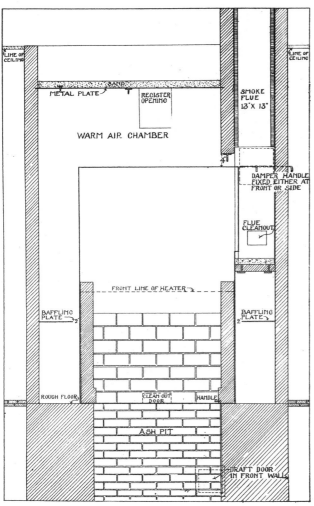

LINE OF CEILING

METAL PLATE

SAND

REGISTER OPENING

SMOKE FLUE 13"X 13"

LINE OF CEILING

WARM AIR CHAMBER

4"

DAMPER HANDLE FIXED EITHER AT FRONT OR SIDE

FLUE CLEANOUT

FRONT LINE OF HEATER

BAFFLING PLATE 2"

BAFFLING PLATE 2"

ROUGH FLOOR

CLEAN OUT DOOR

HANDLE

ASH PIT

DRAFT DOOR IN FRONT WALL

FIG. 2: LONGITUDINAL VERTICAL SECTION THROUGH CRAFTSMAN FIREPLACE.

ing the leg of the chimney below the flue free for the circulation of air.

A rectangular clean-out opening, 4 by 6 inches, is provided at the bottom of the flue, covered by a removable cap placed in the rear wall of the chimneypiece. This allows the soot which falls to the bottom of the flue to be removed from the room behind the fireplace.

A damper is provided in the metal flue directly above its connection with the heater body. This damper may be operated by a rod projecting through the front, side or back of the chimneypiece, as preferred.

When it is desirable to carry the pipe from the kitchen range into the flue of the fireplace, it should be connected above the metal flue so as to be above the damper just described.

When an ash pit is built, a draft door is provided in the wall of the pit close to the cellar ceiling. This door is operated by a small rod projecting up through the hearth, close to the wall.

By means of this draft door and the damper in the flue, the fire can be kept under complete control so that it will hold over night the same as a fire in a furnace.

61

THE CRAFTSMAN FIREPLACE

HOW THE CRAFTSMAN FIRE-PLACE OPERATES

THE operation of the Craftsman fire-place is as follows: As shown in Figure 1, the gases generated by the fire pass up into the combustion chamber, down behind the smoke wall to the bottom of the heater, then under and up behind the inner air chamber to the top of the heater, where they pass through the smoke outlet shown in Figure 4 and out through the chimney.

The air is warmed by the iron walls of the heater and is thus caused to rise and pass up into the warm-air chamber. This action draws in outside air through the fresh-air inlet, and at the same time draws in air from the room through the registers at the base of the fireplace.

The natural tendency of the air drawn in through these registers would be to rise, as it became warmer, direct to the top of the warm-air chamber, without first passing through the air passages of the heater. To prevent the air from making this "short cut" and to ensure its being properly warmed by thorough circulation through the heater, a horizontal baffling plate is provided in each leg of the chimney-piece just above the lower register, to direct the in-drawn air close against the heater and into the air passages.

The warm air is distributed throughout the house as previously explained, the dimensions of pipes and registers being proportioned so that the proper amount of air will be delivered to the various-sized rooms.

The warm air, being the lightest, naturally rises and spreads over the ceiling in even layers, gradually dropping to the floor as it cools, and its place is taken by more warm air. A space of at least half an inch should be left beneath the doors of the rooms so that the air may pass out to the room in which the fireplace is built, to complete the circulation. Part of this air is drawn into the fire and passes out through the chimney, and the rest is drawn into the lower registers as described.

The circulation is constant and positive, being accomplished by gravitation, the heavier or colder air seeking the lower level, and the

THE CRAFTSMAN FIREPLACE

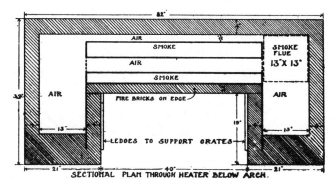

FIG. 3: HORIZONTAL SECTION THROUGH CRAFTSMAN FIREPLACE.

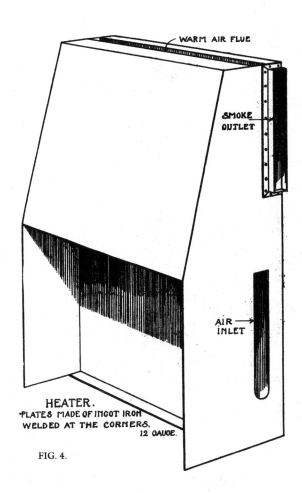

lighter or warmer air the higher level. A continual circulation is thus maintained between the various rooms as well as a movement of the air within the rooms, making a given air supply go much farther than with other heating systems.

During this circulation, the air absorbs all impurities, and naturally the zone of the most vitiated air is nearest the floor. It is from this zone that the fireplace draws its air and discharges it through the chimney.

THE CRAFTSMAN FIREPLACE

Doors and windows should be kept closed in order that the circulation of air may not be disturbed, for upon the proper circulation depends the efficient heating and ventilating of the house. Under these conditions, there can be no drafts.

GUARANTEE

WHEN the installation of a Craftsman fireplace is being considered, I require the floor plans of the house to be sent me. The owner should mark on the plans the points of the compass, and should state whether any of the rooms have a particularly cold or windy exposure.

If, upon examining the plans, I find that my heating system is suitable, I make without charge a layout showing the location and size of warm-air pipes and registers. I also furnish complete working drawings and instructions so that any competent mason can make the installation.

As the fireplace is sold only under these conditions, direct to the user, I guarantee it to furnish proper heat and ventilation wherever it is installed in strict accordance with my directions.

Plans and Illustrations

A CRAFTSMAN CEMENT BUNGALOW FOR SUMMER USE

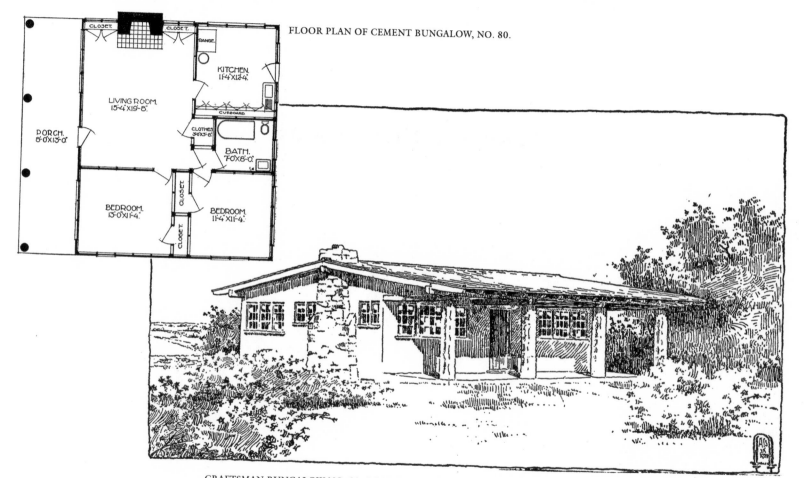

FLOOR PLAN OF CEMENT BUNGALOW, NO. 80.

CLOSET. CLOSET.

RANGE.

KITCHEN.
11'-4" X 12'-4".

LIVING ROOM.
15'-4" X 19'-8".

CUPBOARD.

PORCH.
8'-0" X 13'-0".

CLOTHES.
3'-6" X 3'-6".

BATH.
7'-0" X 8'-0".

BEDROOM.
13'-0" X 11'-4".

CLOSET.

CLOSET.

BEDROOM.
11'-4" X 11'-4".

CRAFTSMAN BUNGALOW NO. 80: A PRACTICAL, COMFORTABLE HOME FOR SUMMER OR FOR WEEK-ENDS.

A CRAFTSMAN CEMENT BUNGALOW FOR SUMMER USE

ALTHOUGH so simple in construction that the owner can assist in building it, this little bungalow will prove a well-planned, serviceable and attractive dwelling. The walls and partitions are of cement mortar upon metal lath. The girders of the house are supported upon concrete piers, less expensive than a stone foundation. The base of the chimney runs to the depth of the piers. The porch floor may be of cinder concrete, the same as used for sidewalks, slightly slanted so that it will drain easily, and the porch roof supports are of logs. The rafters are sheathed with V-jointed boards, dressed, and finished on the under side. These boards make the only ceiling to the cottage, and above them are laid strips of Ruberoid roofing. Within, all the structural beams are left exposed, and are smoothed and stained.

The big chimney in the living room contains also the flue of the kitchen range. Besides these two rooms there are two bedrooms, a bathroom and many convenient closets, the arrangement, as the floor plan shows, being both compact and comfortable.

The groups of windows with their small square panes not only add a touch of interest to the plain cement walls of the building, but give ample air and sunshine to each one of the five rooms within.

In spite of the extreme simplicity of its construction and layout of the interior—or perhaps we should rather say because of this simplicity—the bungalow, when comfortably and tastefully furnished, should make a very charming little summer home, and would certainly permit a minimizing of all housework.

CRAFTSMAN SHINGLED BUNGALOW WITH ROOMY INTERIOR

CONSTRUCTED entirely of dressed lumber, with rough stone for the foundation and chimney, with hewn posts, shingled walls and boarded gables, this bungalow has sufficient of the rustic character to harmonize with its surroundings of wood and mountain.

Casement windows are used, with small panes, and where the windows are not sufficiently sheltered by the roof they are hooded at the top by springing out a row of shingles. Upon the grouping of the windows depends much of the attraction of this very simple exterior.

On entering the living room, the open shelves of books, the fireplace nook with comfortable cushioned seats, and the china closet and wide sideboard in the dining room present an interesting picture. So many pieces have been built in that only a table and a few chairs are necessary to complete the furnishing.

Especially interesting is the arrangement of bedrooms and bath.

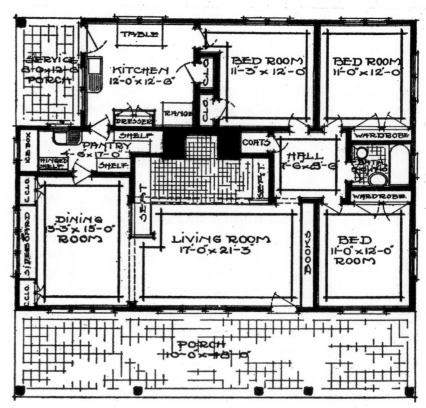

FLOOR PLAN OF HOUSE NO. 116.

CRAFTSMAN SHINGLED BUNGALOW WITH ROOMY INTERIOR

CRAFTSMAN SHINGLED BUNGALOW OF SIMPLE CONSTRUCTION AND UNUSUALLY INTERESTING PLAN, NO. 116: A VIEW OF THE INTERIOR IS SHOWN ON PAGE 26.

SIX-ROOM CRAFTSMAN COTTAGE FOR NARROW LOT

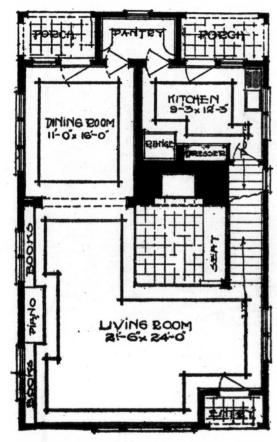

FLOOR PLANS OF COTTAGE NO. 118.

THIS CRAFTSMAN CEMENT COTTAGE, NO. 118, IS PLANNED FOR A NARROW LOT AND IS ONLY A STORY AND A HALF HIGH: DORMERS ARE USED IN FRONT AND REAR: THE FLOOR PLANS ARE ESPECIALLY INTERESTING, THE LOWER FLOOR BEING UNUSUALLY SPACIOUS FOR SO SMALL A HOUSE, AND THE UPPER FLOOR BEING EXTREMELY COMPACT IN ARRANGEMENT: ON PAGE 25 IS SHOWN A VIEW OF THE FIREPLACE CORNER.

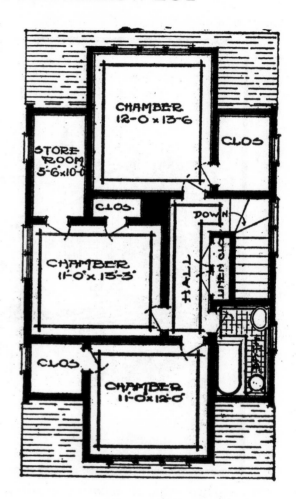

SIX-ROOM CRAFTSMAN COTTAGE FOR NARROW LOT

INEXPENSIVE CRAFTSMAN BUNGALOW OF CEMENT

CRAFTSMAN BUNGALOW NO. 123: THE PERGOLA AND TRELLIS ARE PRACTICAL AS WELL AS DECORATIVE FEATURES OF THIS VERY SIMPLE EXTERIOR.

INEXPENSIVE CRAFTSMAN BUNGALOW OF CEMENT

PLANNED for a small family and designed for a narrow suburban lot, this little bungalow may be inexpensively and yet substantially built. Cement plaster with boarded gable and slate roof are the materials shown here, although concrete foundation and shingled sides and roof might be used; but the durability of cement would more than compensate for its greater initial cost.

The veranda floor may be of concrete, and the pillars of concrete or rough hand-hewn logs. The trellis and the pergola entrance add a decorative note which is pleasing both before the vines have grown and when they are leafless during winter.

The floor plan shows a small but comfortable interior, comprising a large sitting room to be used as a dining room, and two bedrooms, a bathroom and kitchen. Ample closet space is allowed and the kitchen is equipped with all the necessary conveniences. The bungalow can be well warmed and ventilated by the centrally located Craftsman fireplace-furnace.

This plan, like all Craftsman designs, could be modified to suit various requirements. For instance, if the owner happened to need three bedrooms instead of two, another could be added on the right, using some of the space now occupied by the porch. The built-in seat and closets now indicated would then be included in the front bedroom.

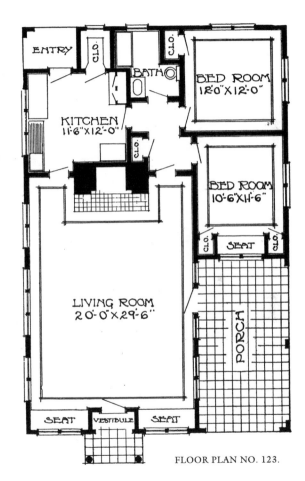

FLOOR PLAN NO. 123.

73

CRAFTSMAN BUNGALOW FOR SIMPLE HOUSEKEEPING

IN the cottage shown here, split stone is used for the walls and for the parapet and pillars of the front porch. The steps and floor of this porch are of cement. The gables are shingled with split cypress shingles, and the roof is also shingled, with the rafters left exposed at the widely overhanging eaves.

The open arrangement of dining room, sitting room and fireplace nook is particularly attractive, and the small hall gives access to the two bedrooms and bath as well as kitchen, dining room and cellar stairs.

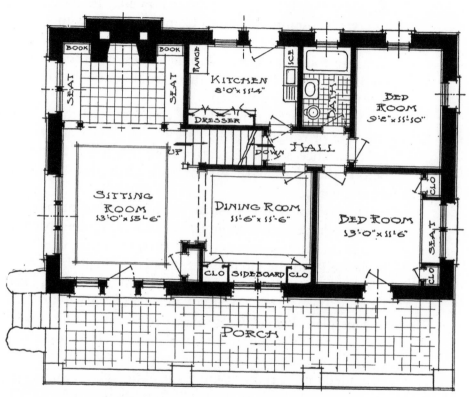

FLOOR PLAN OF CRAFTSMAN BUNGALOW NO. 93.

CRAFTSMAN BUNGALOW FOR SIMPLE HOUSEKEEPING

A CRAFTSMAN FIELD-STONE BUNGALOW WITH SHINGLED ROOF AND GABLES: NO. 93: THIS HOMELIKE BUILDING WAS PLANNED FOR A SLIGHTLY SLOPING SITE, BUT IT COULD EASILY BE ADAPTED TO LEVEL GROUND: THE INTERIOR IS PARTICULARLY WORTH NOTING, AS IT IS BOTH ROOMY AND COMFORTABLE, AND YET SO COMPACT THAT HOUSE-KEEPING WILL BE COMPARATIVELY SIMPLE.

A SEVEN-ROOM CRAFTSMAN CEMENT HOUSE

CEMENT on metal lath was chosen for the construction of this house, because these materials have proven both durable and inexpensive. The long roof lines, stone chimney, recessed porches and small-paned windows are practical and interesting features of the exterior.

A study of the floor plans will also show how close is the relation between an economical arrangement and a comfortable, beautiful home.

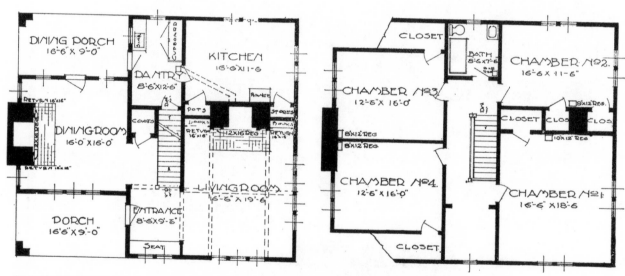

CRAFTSMAN HOUSE NO. 125: FIRST FLOOR PLAN.

NO. 125: SECOND FLOOR PLAN.

A SEVEN-ROOM CRAFTSMAN CEMENT HOUSE

CRAFTSMAN CEMENT HOUSE NO. 125: A PRACTICAL CONSTRUCTION THAT RESULTED IN CONSIDERABLE HOME-
LIKE CHARM WITHOUT ANY ATTEMPT AT DECORATION.

CRAFTSMAN CONCRETE BUNGALOW OF ECONOMICAL DESIGN

IN bungalow No. 131 the entrance door leads from the recessed corner porch, with its concrete pillars, parapets and flower-boxes, directly into the spacious living room, made cheerful by three pleasant window groups and by the welcome vista of the inglenook at the farther end.

From the dining room, through another wide opening, a glimpse is also had of this pleasant nook, with its open hearth, built-in bookshelves and fireside seats, so that both rooms share its comfort and friendliness.

An interesting feature of the left-hand fireside seat is the fact that it may serve as a storage place for coal, which may be put in from the kitchen and taken out in the nook as needed for the fire.

The arrangement of kitchen and rear porches, as well as that of the bedrooms and bath, will be found very convenient.

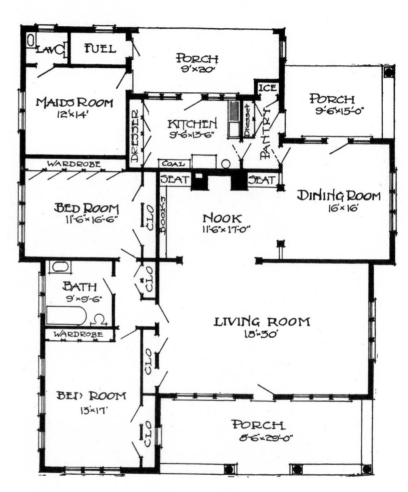

FLOOR PLAN OF CONCRETE BUNGALOW NO. 131.

CRAFTSMAN CONCRETE BUNGALOW OF ECONOMICAL DESIGN

CRAFTSMAN BUNGALOW NO. 131.

SEVEN-ROOM CRAFTSMAN BUNGALOW FOR COUNTRY SITE

THIS bungalow has been planned with care for indoor and outdoor comfort. We have chosen shingles for the walls and roof, but the design would lend itself equally well to other materials.

The chimney is brick and the pillars of the porches are rough hewn from ordinary logs— a little touch that adds to the rustic effect.

The floor plan is well worth studying, for it is so simple, roomy and compact that house-keeping would be a comparatively simple matter.

The wide opening between dining room and large living room adds to the friendliness of the interior, and the sleeping portion of the bungalow is conveniently separated from the rest by the small hall.

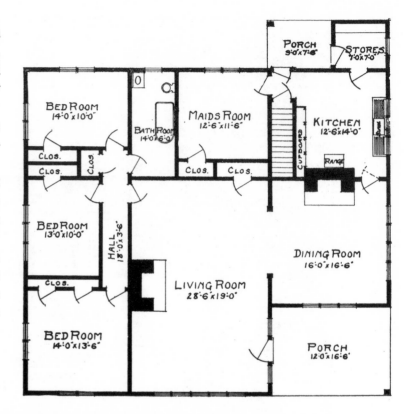

SEVEN-ROOM CRAFTSMAN BUNGALOW FOR COUNTRY SITE

EXTERIOR VIEW AND FLOOR PLAN OF CRAFTSMAN SHINGLED BUNGALOW NO. 140: BOTH THE CONSTRUCTION AND LAYOUT OF THIS COUNTRY HOME ARE WORTH STUDYING.

COMFORTABLE CRAFTSMAN COTTAGE WITH SEVEN ROOMS

T HE interior of this cottage is very compactly planned. The living room with its big stone fireplace occupies one whole side of the house, and is connected with the dining room by the wide, open hall.

One of the bedrooms has an open fireplace with a closet on one side, and in the recess formed by the front dormer there is a long seat built in beneath the window group. A similar seat is provided in the dormer nook in the other front bedroom, and also in one of the rooms at the rear.

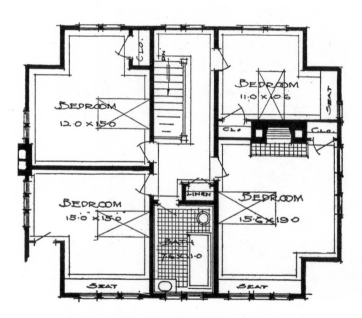

COTTAGE NO. 78: FIRST FLOOR PLAN.

COTTAGE NO. 78: SECOND FLOOR PLAN.

COMFORTABLE CRAFTSMAN COTTAGE WITH SEVEN ROOMS

CRAFTSMAN COTTAGE NO. 78: THE LINES AND PROPORTIONS OF THIS BUILDING AND VARIETY OF MATERIALS USED, MAKE THE EXTERIOR AS PICTURESQUE AS IT IS PRACTICAL.

CRAFTSMAN STUCCO HOUSE WITH PORCHES AND BALCONY

THIS house is so well adapted to the material chosen here—stucco on metal lath—that we would suggest that either this or concrete be used.

The sheltered porches, the pleasant window groups, the long sloping roof broken by the dormer with its protecting overhang, and the sunken balcony with its little parapet combine to give the exterior its air of quiet dignity and charm.

The small recessed porch, the open hallway, built-in seat and pleasant staircase make the entrance unusually attractive.

The living room and dining room both have glass doors opening onto the big living porch at the side, and the rest of the lower floor is taken up by a well-equipped pantry and kitchen.

The upstairs plan is very compact and simple, and the irregular shape of the bedrooms will add to the interest of the furnishings.

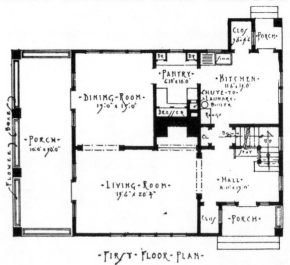

-FIRST-FLOOR-PLAN-

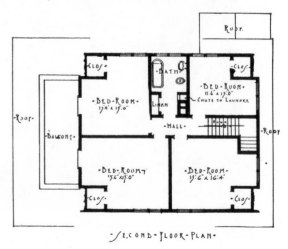

-SECOND-FLOOR-PLAN-

CRAFTSMAN STUCCO HOUSE WITH PORCHES AND BALCONY

CRAFTSMAN STUCCO HOUSE NO. 149: THE ROOMS WITHIN ARE AS SIMPLE AND HOMELIKE AS THE EXTERIOR.

AN EIGHT-ROOM CRAFTSMAN FARMHOUSE

CEMENT on metal lath is suggested for the construction of this house, the general lines of which are similar to those of an old-fashioned New England farmhouse. The four-foot overhang at the eaves, the supporting brackets, the chimneys at each side, the corner porch and entrance pergola are all practical and interesting features of the exterior.

The first floor plan with its open arrangement of hall, living room, den and stairs, is exceptionally attractive, and the staircase, which can be reached from both hall and dining room, gives opportunity for a decorative use of the necessary woodwork.

A recessed sleeping porch and a couple of window-seats add to the comfort of the second floor.

NO. 74. FIRST FLOOR PLAN.

NO. 74. SECOND FLOOR PLAN.

AN EIGHT-ROOM CRAFTSMAN FARMHOUSE

CRAFTSMAN FARMHOUSE NO. 74: THE INTERIOR IS DELIGHTFULLY ROOMY, COMFORTABLE AND COMPACT IN ARRANGEMENT.

CRAFTSMAN HOUSE PLANNED FOR MUCH OUTDOOR LIFE

CRAFTSMAN STUCCO HOUSE NO. 114: THIS SIMPLE EXTERIOR DEPENDS FOR ITS STRUCTURAL INTEREST ON THE CAREFULLY GROUPED WINDOWS AND THE ARRANGEMENT OF PORCHES AND SLEEPING BALCONIES: THE FLOOR PLANS, WHICH ARE AS CONVENIENT AND COMPACT AS POSSIBLE, AFFORD AMPLE OPPORTUNITY FOR BOTH HOSPITALITY AND PRIVACY.

CRAFTSMAN HOUSE PLANNED FOR MUCH OUTDOOR LIFE

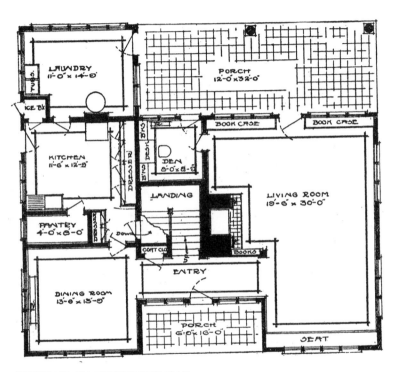

HOUSE NO. 114: FIRST FLOOR PLAN.

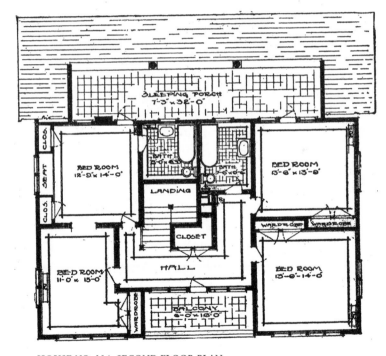

HOUSE NO. 114: SECOND FLOOR PLAN.

CRAFTSMAN BUNGALOW WITH PORCHES AND OPEN COURT

THE floor plan of this bungalow has been worked out so as to utilize all the space to the best possible advantage.

The open arrangement of living and dining rooms, with their pleasant window groups, fireplaces and bookshelves, adds to the feeling of spaciousness indoors, while the sheltered court in the rear affords a delightful place for outdoor living and brings the home into close contact with the garden.

The layout of kitchen, maid's room, pantry, etc., is very compact and convenient, and the sleeping rooms on the other side of the plan are equally shut off from the living rooms.

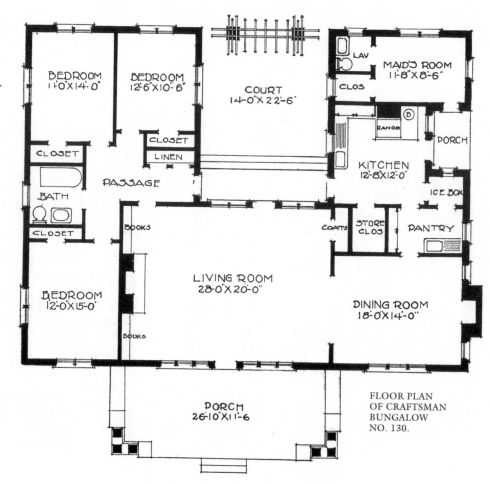

FLOOR PLAN
OF CRAFTSMAN
BUNGALOW
NO. 130.

CRAFTSMAN BUNGALOW WITH PORCHES AND OPEN COURT

CRAFTSMAN BUNGALOW NO. 130, SHOWING INTERESTING USE OF BRICK, FIELD STONE AND STRUCTURAL BEAMS.

COMPACTLY PLANNED EIGHT-ROOM CRAFTSMAN HOUSE

CRAFTSMAN HOUSE NO. 146: CONCRETE IS USED FOR THE WALLS AND SHINGLES FOR THE ROOF, WHILE FIELD STONE AND BRICK GIVE A TOUCH OF VARIETY TO PERGOLA, CHIMNEY AND GARDEN WALL. THE FLOOR PLANS BELOW SHOW A SIMPLE, CONVENIENT ARRANGEMENT OF ROOMS, WHICH SHOULD PROVE VERY HOMELIKE AND LIVABLE.

COMPACTLY PLANNED EIGHT-ROOM CRAFTSMAN HOUSE

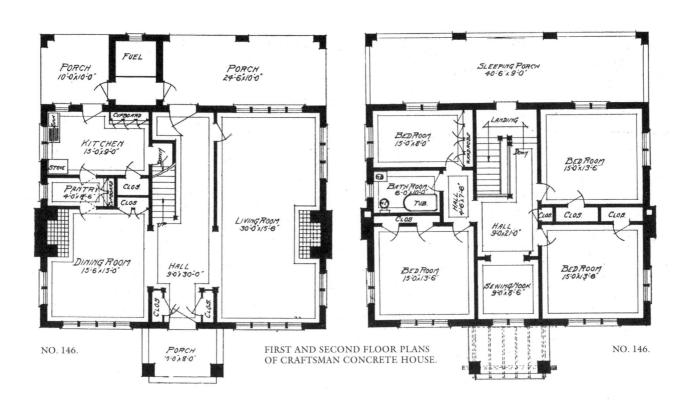

PORCH
10'-0"x10'-0"

FUEL

PORCH
24'-6"x10'-0"

CUPBOARD

KITCHEN
15'-0"x9'-0"

STOVE

PANTRY
4'-0"x8'-6"

CLOS

CLOS

LIVING ROOM
30'-0"x15'-6"

DINING ROOM
15'-6"x15'-0"

HALL
9'-0"x30'-0"

CLOS

CLOS

NO. 146.

PORCH
7'-0"x8'-0"

FIRST AND SECOND FLOOR PLANS
OF CRAFTSMAN CONCRETE HOUSE.

NO. 146.

SLEEPING PORCH
40'-6"x9'-0"

BED ROOM
15'-0"x8'-0"

LANDING

DOWN

WARDROBE

BED ROOM
15'-0"x13'-6"

BATH ROOM
6'-0"x10'-0"

TUB.

HALL
4'-6"x7'-6"

CLOS.

CLOS.

CLOS.

CLOS.

BED ROOM
15'-0"x13'-6"

SEWING NOOK
9'-0"x8'-6"

HALL
9'-0"x21'-0"

BED ROOM
15'-0"x13'-6"

NINE-ROOM CRAFTSMAN COTTAGE OF BRICK AND SHINGLES

CRAFTSMAN BRICK COTTAGE NO. 135: PLANNED FOR COMFORT, CONVENIENCE AND ECONOMY.

THIS cottage is a story and a half high, the rooms on the second floor being given sufficient height by the dormer which breaks the rather steep slope of the roof and adds to the interest of the exterior.

The building is set very close to the ground, on a foundation of field stone, thus emphasizing its friendly relation to the surrounding landscape.

In addition to the large living room and dining room, there is a den at the

NINE-ROOM CRAFTSMAN COTTAGE OF BRICK AND SHINGLES

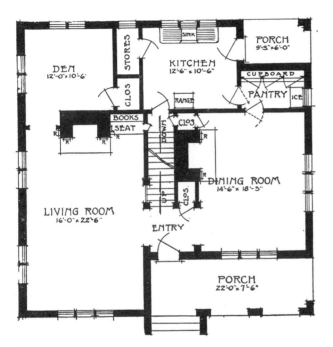

HOUSE NO. 135: FIRST FLOOR PLAN.

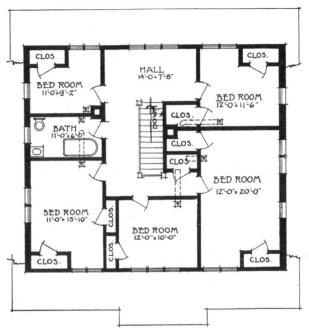

HOUSE NO. 135: SECOND FLOOR PLAN.

rear, which can be shut off from the rest of the house, affording a quiet place for work or rest.

A small porch is provided off the kitchen, sheltered by the walls and overhanging roof.

Upstairs there are five good-sized bedrooms and bath, each opening out of a central hall which is well lighted and ventilated by a group of windows.

TWO SHINGLED HOUSES OF TYPICAL CRAFTSMAN DESIGN

THE ABOVE CRAFTSMAN HOUSE, NO. 155, COMPRISES A LARGE LIVING ROOM AND DINING ROOM, KITCHEN, PANTRY AND LAVATORY DOWNSTAIRS, AND FOUR BEDROOMS ON THE SECOND FLOOR, IN ADDITION TO DRESSING ROOM, MAID'S ROOM, TOILET, BATH AND SLEEPING PORCH: FLOOR PLANS WILL BE FOUND IN THE CRAFTSMAN FOR MARCH, 1913.

TWO SHINGLED HOUSES OF TYPICAL CRAFTSMAN DESIGN

HOUSE NO. 156, ILLUSTRATED ABOVE, CONTAINS DOWNSTAIRS A LARGE LIVING ROOM, DINING ROOM, HALL, DRESSING ROOM, KITCHEN, PANTRY, FUEL SHED, ONE FRONT AND TWO REAR PORCHES, AND A TERRACE AT THE SIDE: UPSTAIRS ARE FOUR BEDROOMS, TWO BATHROOMS, MAID'S ROOM AND MAID'S BATHROOM, WITH PLENTY OF STORAGE SPACE: FOR FLOOR PLANS, SEE THE CRAFTSMAN FOR MARCH, 1913.

CRAFTSMAN HOUSE WITH INGLENOOK AND BUILT-IN FITTINGS

THE long sloping roofs of shingle or slate, in which dormers are built to give height to the upper rooms, make the exterior of this cement house especially satisfying. The building is strongly constructed upon truss metal lath, and the cement is brought close about the windows, which are so grouped as to break the wall into pleasing spaces.

The many built-in fittings will make the living and dining rooms extremely interesting as well as convenient, and the seats built-in beneath the bedroom windows will add to the homelike atmosphere upstairs. In fact, the house, if built as designed here, will require very little furnishing.

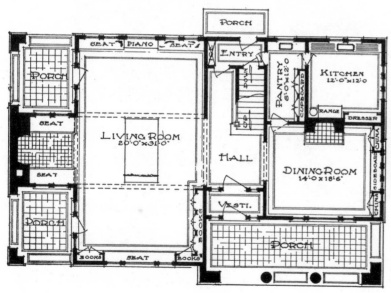

HOUSE NO. 79: FIRST FLOOR PLAN.

HOUSE NO. 79: SECOND FLOOR PLAN.

CRAFTSMAN HOUSE WITH INGLENOOK AND BUILT-IN FITTINGS

TYPICAL CRAFTSMAN CEMENT HOUSE, WITH EIGHT ROOMS, COSY FIREPLACE NOOK AND THREE PORCHES: NO. 79.

ELEVEN-ROOM CRAFTSMAN HOUSE

CEMENT HOUSE NO. 154: IN ADDITION TO THE ROOMS SHOWN IN THE TWO FLOOR PLANS BELOW, THERE ARE ALSO TWO BEDROOMS, A SEWING ROOM, BATHROOM AND FOUR STORAGE PLACES IN THE ATTIC: COMPLETE PLANS WERE PUBLISHED IN THE CRAFTSMAN FOR FEBRUARY, 1913.

ELEVEN-ROOM CRAFTSMAN HOUSE

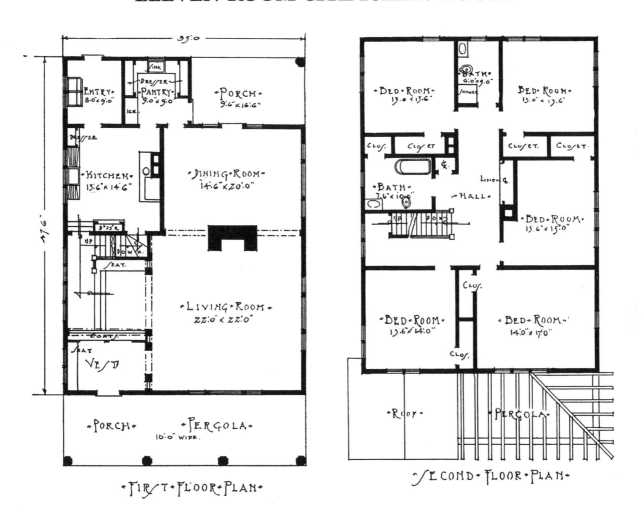

·FIR/T·FLOOR·PLAN·

·/ECOND·FLOOR·PLAN·

101

ELEVEN-ROOM CRAFTSMAN BRICK HOUSE

A YEAR ago, in Washington, was built one of the most successful and certainly the largest and most completely modern of all our Craftsman houses—"Dumblane," which we are illustrating on page 110.

This Southern home has proved a source of so much genuine comfort and enjoyment to its owners and satisfaction to ourselves, and has met with such keen appreciation from architects and laymen alike, that we have naturally wanted to design another along somewhat similar lines. But the majority of home-builders, of course, would find such a residence too large as well as too elaborate and expensive for their needs, and so we have worked out a plan which embodies on a smaller scale some of the most attractive features of "Dumblane's" arrangement and design, and is at the same time sufficiently economical in construction to be within reach of moderate incomes. The result of our effort is shown here, in Craftsman House No. 153.

The exterior of the building is decidedly reminiscent of its larger predecessor. Its two and a half stories, with brick walls and shingled roof, have the same general outlines and solidity of proportion; while the inviting shelter of the long pergolas, the glass conservatory at the side, the pleasant groups of windows, the three dormers that break the roof lines in front and rear, are all features which "Dumblane" and the present house share. And the interior of the latter, though different in the details of its planning, holds the same charm of wide spaces and airy, well-lighted rooms that characterizes the larger residence.

As to the materials of House No. 153—"Tapestry" brick will of course give the richest and most distinctive effect; but if this cannot be had, very pleasing results can be obtained with ordinary clinker brick, provided good judgment is used in selection and laying.

A practical point worth noting is the arrangement of the pergolas and porches so that sufficient shelter is provided without cutting off too much light from the windows. In front, the entrance portion is roofed over, and

ELEVEN-ROOM CRAFTSMAN BRICK HOUSE

EXTERIOR VIEW OF CRAFTSMAN HOUSE NO. 153: PLANS ON PAGES 104-105.

ELEVEN-ROOM CRAFTSMAN BRICK HOUSE

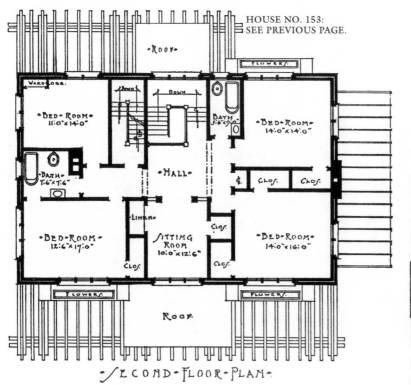

HOUSE NO. 153:
SEE PREVIOUS PAGE.

·SECOND·FLOOR·PLAN·

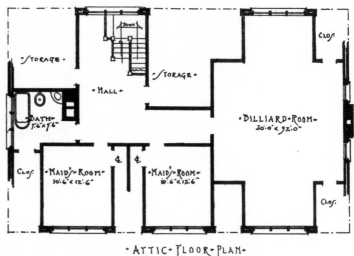

·ATTIC·FLOOR·PLAN·

HOUSE NO. 153: SEE PREVIOUS PAGE.

104

ELEVEN-ROOM CRAFTSMAN BRICK HOUSE

in the rear the same construction is used at the hall door.

The floor plans will be found well worth studying. Downstairs the arrangement is very open, the only divisions between the hall, living room and dining room being the projecting vestibule and the post-and-panel construction between the living-room fireplace and the stairs.

The built-in seats and bookcases add to the comfort and structural interest of the interior, and the glass doors that open onto the pergola and conservatory make the rooms unusually light and cheerful.

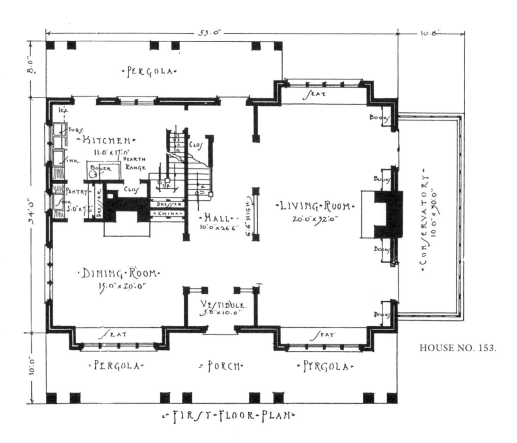

HOUSE NO. 153.

TWO-FAMILY CRAFTSMAN CEMENT HOUSE

THE two-family house shown here may be of concrete or stucco, with shingled roof. While brick could be substituted if desired, the general form and lines of the structure seem to lend themselves best to concrete or stucco construction.

The symmetrical arrangement of the exterior, combined with its solid, well balanced proportions, give the place an air of dignity without being at all severe; while the inviting shelter of the recessed entrance porches and those on each side, and the small dormers and sunken balconies that break the slope of the long roofs, contribute to the homelike appearance of the building.

In looking over the floor plans, let us take the left-hand house. One enters from the small loggia, which may be either divided from its neighbor by a full or half-height partition or left open for greater space and friendliness.

In the roomy hall one finds a hospitable seat beside the staircase, which goes up three steps to a landing before turning up to the second floor.

A double closet which may serve for wraps and umbrellas is conveniently near, and through it one may pass to the kitchen—an arrangement which allows the maid or housewife to answer the front door or run upstairs without disturbing the people in the living room.

Through the wide opening on the left one has a glimpse of the fireplace nook, recessed sufficiently to emphasize its cosiness, yet not enough to shut it off from the rest of the room. Glass doors open onto the porch, which is so well protected from sun and rain that it will prove a popular place for outdoor living.

The dining room, which is comfortably large and lighted by pleasant window groups overlooking the garden, communicates with a small pantry equipped with dressers and shelves. By placing the pantry window rather high in the wall, room may be left below for the ice-box, which may be filled through a door from the kitchen porch. The kitchen is fairly large, and from it the cellar

TWO-FAMILY CRAFTSMAN CEMENT HOUSE

A TWO-FAMILY CRAFTSMAN HOUSE, AFFORDING AN OPPORTUNITY FOR ECONOMY OF CONSTRUCTION WITHOUT LOSS OF ARCHITECTURAL BEAUTY: NO. 151: SEE FLOOR PLANS ON PAGES 108-109.

TWO-FAMILY CRAFTSMAN CEMENT HOUSE

stairs descend below the main staircase.

The second floor comprises four bedrooms and bathroom, all opening out of the central hall and being provided with fair-sized closets. The small sunken balcony referred to before will afford a place for ferns or flower boxes that will add a note of cheeriness to the outlook from the largest bedroom.

These plans can of course be modified to suit individual needs. For example, if the

SEE PAGE 107.

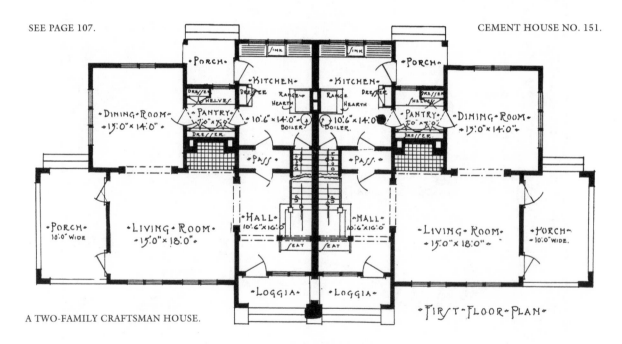

CEMENT HOUSE NO. 151.

A TWO-FAMILY CRAFTSMAN HOUSE.

·FIRST·FLOOR·PLAN·

TWO-FAMILY CRAFTSMAN CEMENT HOUSE

owner preferred to have a larger living room, the partition between that room and the hall might be omitted, and the division merely indicated by post-and-panel construction. Or the butler's pantry might be dispensed with and the size of kitchen, dining room or porch increased by a rearrangement of partitions; in which case a storage pantry or cupboard could be provided in some convenient corner near the kitchen.

SEE PAGE 107.

CEMENT HOUSE NO. 151.

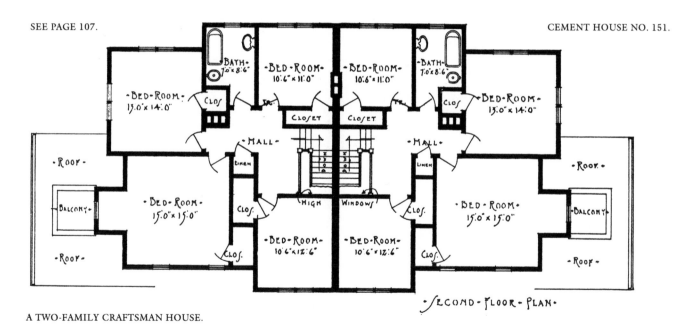

A TWO-FAMILY CRAFTSMAN HOUSE.

·SECOND·FLOOR·PLAN·

109

HOMES BUILT FROM CRAFTSMAN DESIGNS

"DUMBLANE," THE CRAFTSMAN HOME OF MR. AND MRS. S. HAZEN BOND, NEAR WASHINGTON, D. C., ILLUSTRATIONS, PLANS AND DESCRIPTION OF WHICH WERE PUBLISHED IN THE CRAFTSMAN FOR FEBRUARY, 1913.

HOMES BUILT FROM CRAFTSMAN DESIGNS

ONE END OF THE FRIENDLY DINING ROOM IN THE BOND HOUSE, SHOWING VARIOUS CRAFTSMAN FITTINGS AND FURNITURE AND A TYPICAL CRAFTSMAN TREATMENT OF THE WOODWORK.

HOMES BUILT FROM CRAFTSMAN DESIGNS

THE CRAFTSMAN HOUSE ESPECIALLY DESIGNED FOR MR. F. S. PEER OF ITHACA, N. Y.: AN INTERESTING
EXAMPLE OF STUCCO AND HALF-TIMBER CONSTRUCTION.

HOMES BUILT FROM CRAFTSMAN DESIGNS

THE HOME OF MR. ARCHER H. BARBER, NORTH ADAMS, MASS., BUILT AFTER A CRAFTSMAN DESIGN: THE
HOUSE IS ON A HILLSIDE AND IS SO PLANNED THAT IT ACCOMMODATES ITSELF TO EVERY IRREGULARITY IN
THE SITE.

HOMES BUILT FROM CRAFTSMAN DESIGNS

HOUSE AT MAPLEWOOD, N.J., BUILT FOR MR. E. L. PRIOR FROM CRAFTSMAN PLANS: THE COMBINATION OF CONCRETE AND SHINGLES IN THE WALLS AND FIELD STONE AND BRICK IN THE CHIMNEY ADDS TO THE INTEREST OF THE EXTERIOR.

HOMES BUILT FROM CRAFTSMAN DESIGNS

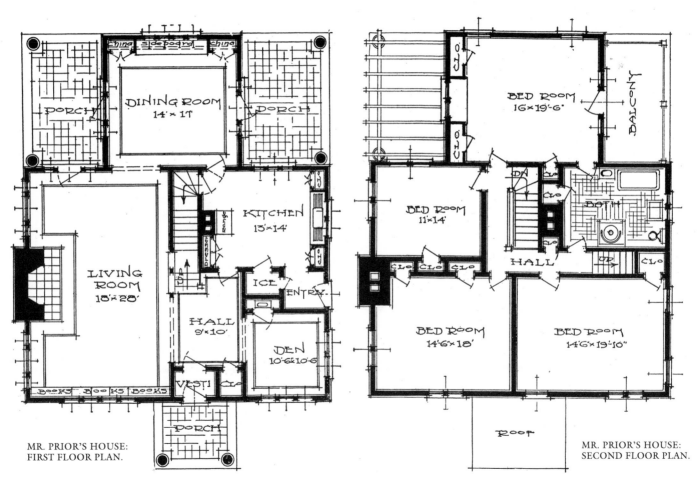

MR. PRIOR'S HOUSE:
FIRST FLOOR PLAN.

MR. PRIOR'S HOUSE:
SECOND FLOOR PLAN.

115

HOMES BUILT FROM CRAFTSMAN DESIGNS

ONE END OF THE LIVING ROOM IN MR. PRIOR'S HOUSE, SHOWING AN INTERESTING ARRANGEMENT OF BUILT-IN BOOKSHELVES AND WINDOWS: THE WOODWORK OF WALLS AND CEILING, THE BRICK CHIMNEY-PIECE AND THE CRAFTSMAN LANTERNS ARE PARTICULARLY PLEASING.

HOMES BUILT FROM CRAFTSMAN DESIGNS

A CORNER OF THE DINING ROOM IN THE PRIOR HOUSE, SHOWING HOW THE END WALL IS FILLED BY A BUILT-IN SIDEBOARD, CHINA CABINETS AND A GROUP OF SMALL-PANED WINDOWS.

HOMES BUILT FROM CRAFTSMAN DESIGNS

THE CRAFTSMAN HOUSE OF MR. B. A. TAYLOR, BEECHWOOD PARK, SUMMIT, N. J., SHOWING ENTRANCE AND LIVING PORCH AT THE SIDE: THIS CEMENT AND SHINGLE HOUSE IS BUILT ON THE TOP OF A SMALL HILL: THE FLOOR PLANS GIVE SOME IDEA OF THE OPPORTUNITY THE INTERIOR AFFORDED FOR AN INTERESTING USE OF WOODWORK AND OTHER STRUCTURAL FEATURES.

HOMES BUILT FROM CRAFTSMAN DESIGNS

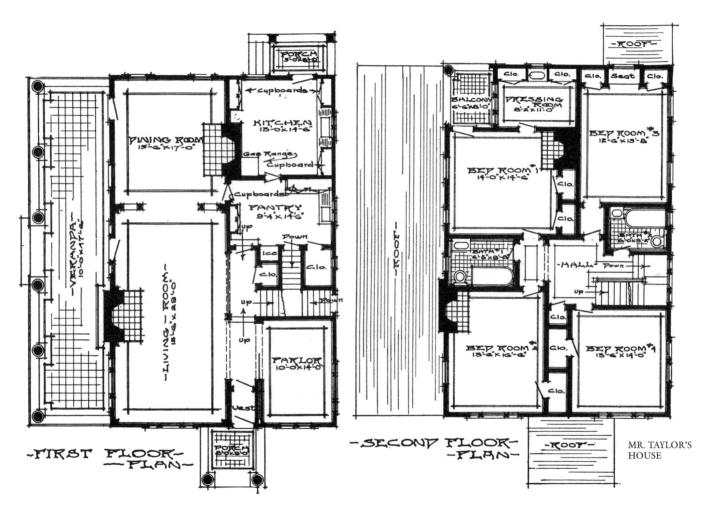

VERANDA
10'-0"x17'-0"

DINING ROOM
15'-6"x17'-0"

KITCHEN
13'-0"x14'-6"

Cupboards

Gas Range
Cupboard

Cupboards

PANTRY
9'-4"x14'-6"

PORCH
3'-0"x6'-0"

Up

Down

Ice

Clo.   Clo.

LIVING ROOM
15'-6"x29'-0"

Up

Up

PARLOR
10'-0"x14'-0"

Clo.

Vest.

~FIRST FLOOR~
~PLAN~

PORCH
8'-0"x6'-0"

ROOF

~ROOF~

BALCONY
6'-6"x8'-0"

DRESSING
ROOM
8'-2"x11'-0"

Clo.   Clo.   Clo.   Seat   Clo.

BED ROOM #3
12'-6"x13'-8"

BED ROOM #1
14'-0"x14'-6"

Clo.

Clo.

BATH
6'-0"x9'-0"

BATH
6'-6"x9'-0"

~HALL~   Down

Up

Clo.

BED ROOM #2
13'-6"x16'-6"

Clo.

BED ROOM #1
13'-6"x14'-0"

Clo.

~SECOND FLOOR~
~PLAN~

~ROOF~

MR. TAYLOR'S
HOUSE

119

HOMES BUILT FROM CRAFTSMAN DESIGNS

BOTH the exterior construction and the interior arrangement of this house are typical examples of the Craftsman idea, while expressing the individual taste of the owner.

The low, broad proportions, the simple roof lines, the pleasant grouping of the windows and the inviting pergola porch that extends entirely across the front of the building, give the place a very homelike air.

The first floor plan shows our characteristic open layout of hall, living room and dining room, and the fireplace with its tiled hearth and comfortable seats forms a cosy retreat without shutting the warmth and beauty of the fire itself from the rest of the downstairs rooms.

In the compact upper story it will be noticed that the corner closets of the largest bedroom provide a charming recess for a built-in window seat.

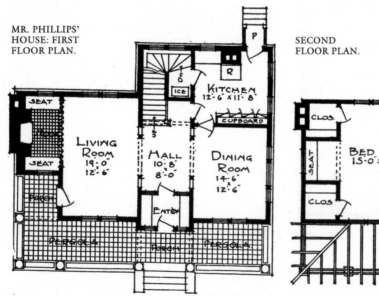

MR. PHILLIPS'
HOUSE: FIRST
FLOOR PLAN.

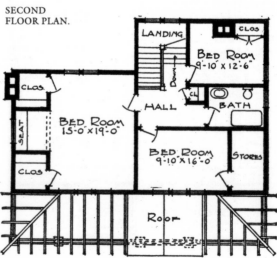

SECOND
FLOOR PLAN.

HOMES BUILT FROM CRAFTSMAN DESIGNS

ANOTHER CRAFTSMAN HOUSE, THE HOME OF MR. W. H. PHILLIPS, WHITESTONE, L. I., SHOWING ENTRANCE THROUGH PERGOLA PORCH.

HOMES BUILT FROM CRAFTSMAN DESIGNS

THE HOME OF MR. S. J. MOORE, POUGHKEEPSIE, N. Y., BUILT FROM A CRAFTSMAN DESIGN.

THE hilltop home illustrated on the left was built of concrete on a foundation of field stone, and the sloping roof is of green slate.

Both the proportions and lines of the exterior and the colors of the various materials used in the construction harmonize admirably with the surrounding landscape, while the winding pathway with its rough stone border links the place even more closely to the hillside.

The long, wide porch, the stone chimney, the dormer and the small-paned casements all add to the friendly air of the building.

HOMES BUILT FROM CRAFTSMAN DESIGNS

THE house shown on the right was built on a hillside, and it would be difficult to imagine a more satisfying and picturesque design or one better adapted to this site.

The construction is frame and wire, plastered with three coats of cement in the natural color. The cypress trimmings are stained brown and the blinds painted green.

As Miss Kakas wrote us, "The house was evolved from long and careful study of the Craftsman designs and planned in every detail to meet the owner's needs."

THE PICTURESQUE HOME OF MISS E. C. KAKAS AT MEDFORD, MASS.

HOMES BUILT FROM CRAFTSMAN DESIGNS

HOUSE AT SLEEPY EYE, MINN., BUILT FROM CRAFTSMAN PLA0NS FOR MR. AND MRS. A. F. STRICKLER.

THE house on the left has been lived in for over six years, and Mrs. Strickler says they are more than satisfied with it.

The walls are of concrete, and the interior is finished throughout with gumwood.

The arrangement of the plans, as in the case of the houses shown above, is very homelike, but space will not permit their reproduction here.

These illustrations, and those on the preceding pages, can give only a general idea of the homes that are constantly being built from our designs.

CRAFTSMAN BUILT-IN FITTINGS AND WOODWORK

THE ABOVE ILLUSTRATION SUGGESTS A PRACTICAL AND PLEASING ARRANGEMENT OF BUILT-IN FITTINGS FOR A TYPICAL CRAFTS-MAN HOME: ON THE LEFT IS THE DINING-ROOM SIDEBOARD WITH CHINA CABINETS ON EITHER HAND: ON THE RIGHT ARE THE LIVING-ROOM DESK AND BOOKCASES, AND IN THE CENTER, IN THE RECESS FORMED BY THESE FITMENTS, IS A COMFORTABLE WIN-DOW-SEAT: THE GROUPS OF SMALL-PANED CASEMENT WINDOWS AND THE SIMPLE WOODWORK OF WALLS AND CEILING ADD TO THE HOMELIKE ATMOSPHERE.

CRAFTSMAN BUILT-IN FITTINGS AND WOODWORK

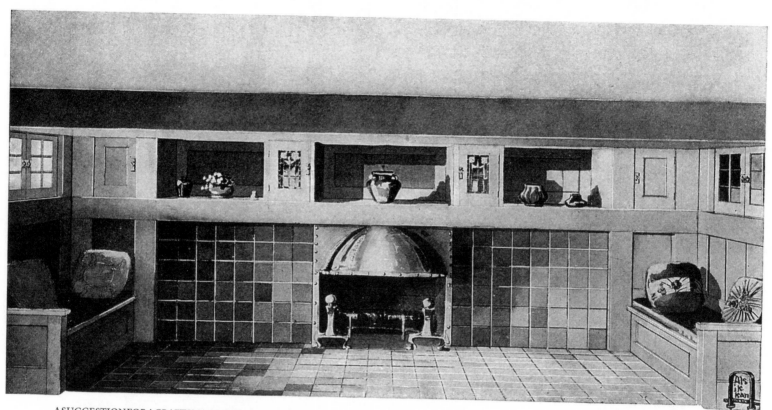

A SUGGESTION FOR A CRAFTSMAN FIREPLACE NOOK IS GIVEN HERE: THE TILED HEARTH AND WALL, THE BUILT-IN SEATS WITH CASEMENTS ABOVE, THE USEFUL CUPBOARDS AND ALCOVES THAT FILL THE SPACE ABOVE THE FIREPLACE, AND THE SOMEWHAT UNIQUE DESIGN OF THE METAL HOOD—ALL THESE ARE PRACTICAL AND AT THE SAME TIME DECORATIVE FEATURES OF THE CONSTRUCTION: THE NOOK AFFORDS A DELIGHTFUL OPPORTUNITY FOR AN EFFECTIVE USE OF COLOR IN TILES, WOODWORK, CUSHIONS AND OTHER DETAILS.

A FEW SUGGESTIONS FROM THE CRAFTSMAN WORKSHOPS

THIS FUMED OAK SETTLE WITH ITS COMFORTABLE
LEATHER CUSHIONS—ONE OF MANY CRAFTSMAN
DESIGNS—WOULD BE A WELCOME ADDITION TO THE
FURNISHINGS OF LIVING ROOM, DEN OR LIBRARY.

THIS IS A TYPICAL CRAFTSMAN CHAIR
THAT WOULD ADD TO THE COMFORT
AND BEAUTY OF ANY INTERIOR.

CATALOGUES OF FURNITURE AND FURNISHINGS SENT ON REQUEST.

A FEW SUGGESTIONS FROM THE CRAFTSMAN WORKSHOPS

THE CHAIR ILLUSTRATED BELOW GIVES SOME IDEA OF THE CHARM OF OUR FIRMLY WOVEN, MELLOW-TONED WILLOW FURNITURE ONE OR TWO OF THESE PIECES FORM A PLEASANT CONTRAST AMONG THE HEAVIER OAK FURNISHINGS.

THIS HEXAGONAL CRAFTSMAN TABLE, WHICH CAN BE HAD WITH WOOD OR HARD LEATHER TOP, IS SUITABLE FOR EITHER LIBRARY OR LIVING ROOM.

CATALOGUES OF FURNITURE AND FURNISHINGS SENT ON REQUEST.

A FEW SUGGESTIONS FROM THE CRAFTSMAN WORKSHOPS

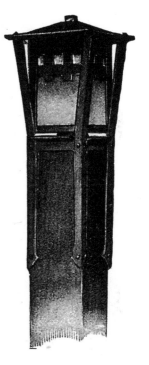

THE NEWEL POST LAMP SHOWN ON THE RIGHT IS ONE OF SEVERAL CRAFTSMAN DESIGNS. LIKE MOST OF OUR LIGHTING FIXTURES, IT COMES IN HAMMERED COPPER, BRASS OR WROUGHT IRON, AND THE LIGHT IS DIFFUSED THROUGH PANELS OF AMBER TINTED HAMMERED GLASS. THIS LAMP WOULD PROVE BOTH PRACTICAL AND BEAUTIFUL AT THE FOOT OF A STAIRCASE, AS SUGGESTED IN SOME OF THE INTERIOR VIEWS IN THIS BOOK.

ONE OF THE SMALLER CRAFTSMAN WRITING DESKS IS SHOWN HERE. ITS SIMPLE DESIGN AND CONVENIENT ARRANGEMENT MAKE IT SUITABLE FOR PRACTICALLY ANY ROOM, EITHER UPSTAIRS OR DOWN.

MUCH OF THE BEAUTY OF A ROOM DEPENDS ON THE LIGHTING FIXTURES. WE MAKE OURS STURDY AND SIMPLE IN CONSTRUCTION, AND ARRANGE THE LIGHT SO THAT IT WILL BE EFFECTIVE AND AT THE SAME TIME RESTFUL TO THE EYES. THE ELECTRIC HANGING LANTERN ON THE LEFT WILL ILLUSTRATE OUR POINT. IT COMES IN HAMMERED COPPER, BRASS OR WROUGHT IRON, AND THE LIGHT IS MELLOWED BY PANELS OF AMBER TINTED GLASS.

CATALOGUES OF FURNITURE AND FURNISHINGS SENT ON REQUEST.

A FEW SUGGESTIONS FROM THE CRAFTSMAN WORKSHOPS

THE ELECTRIC HANGING FIXTURE SHOWN ABOVE COULD BE USED EFFECTIVELY OVER A DINING-ROOM TABLE OR IN A LIVING ROOM OR HALL. THERE ARE FIVE BULBS, FOUR DIFFUSING LIGHT THROUGH THE SILK-LINED WILLOW SHADE, AND ONE THROUGH THE BOWL OF YELLOW LEADED GLASS AT THE BOTTOM.

A CRAFTSMAN THUMB LATCH THAT CAN BE HAD IN COPPER, BRASS OR IRON.

THERE ARE MANY PLACES IN AN INTERIOR WHERE A BRACKET LANTERN IS MORE APPROPRIATE THAN A TABLE OR CEILING LIGHT. ON THE RIGHT IS A SUGGESTION FOR A CRAFTSMAN ELECTRIC BRACKET LANTERN— ONE OF MANY INTERESTING DESIGNS.

CATALOGUES OF FURNITURE AND FURNISHINGS SENT ON REQUEST.

A FEW SUGGESTIONS FROM THE CRAFTSMAN WORKSHOPS

THE SIMPLE, WELL MADE DESK SET SHOWN BELOW COULD BE USED WITH ANY STYLE OF DESK. THE HAMMERED COPPER OR BRASS IS PARTICULARLY PLEASING WITH THE FUMED OAK OF CRAFTSMAN FURNITURE

A CRAFTSMAN
LOCK AND
THUMB-LATCH.

A CANDLESTICK IS ALWAYS A USEFUL AND DELIGHTFUL ADDITION TO A MANTELPIECE OR SHELF. THIS ONE IS MADE IN HAMMERED COPPER, BRASS OR WROUGHT IRON.

THE ONE-LIGHT ELECTRIC LAMP ON THE LEFT IS ESPE-CIALLY SUITABLE FOR DESK OR TABLE USE. THE HAMMERED COPPER OR BRASS STANDARD AND WILLOW SHADE FORM AN UNUSUALLY PLEASING COMBI-NATION, WHETHER THE LAMP IS LIT OR NOT.

CATALOGUES OF FURNITURE AND FURNISHINGS SENT ON REQUEST.

CRAFTSMAN LUSTRE

A Stain, Finish and Polish for all Kinds
of Furniture, Woodwork and Floors · · ·

The home-builder who is called upon to select some kind of wood finish is confronted by an important problem. The whole appearance of the interior of his home hinges on this choice.

There are many different finishes for him to select from, all equally important in their place, but there is only one Craftsman finish, and that is CRAFTSMAN LUSTRE.

This Lustre retains and emphasizes the natural interest and beauty of the wood, while protecting the surface from soil and moisture.

The colored Lustre, which can be had in brown, green, gray and their various modifications, is a stain and polish combined, giving the wood a mellow coloring and finish.

The clear Lustre is a polish, and can be used for all kinds of woodwork, furniture and floors, old or new.

CRAFTSMAN LUSTRE IS VERY EASY TO APPLY.

ITS USE WILL KEEP HARDWOOD FLOORS FRESH AND BRIGHT.

IT WILL REFINISH YOUR FURNITURE AND WOODWORK BEAUTIFULLY.

IT IS USED BY PIANO MANUFACTURERS TO FINISH THEIR CASES.

We believe that a small trial order will convince you of the superiority of Craftsman Lustre. It can be obtained from us by parcels post, or from our associate dealers, a list of whom will be found on the inside front cover.

One gallon covers about 400 square feet as a first coat, and 700 square feet as a second coat.

The prices are as follows:

CLEAR LUSTRE		COLORED LUSTRE	
1 GALLON	$2.00	1 GALLON	$2.50
½ GALLON	$1.10	½ GALLON	$1.40
1 QUART	.60	1 QUART	.75
1 PINT	.35	1 PINT	.45

Send 25 cents for a trial pint can to

GUSTAV STICKLEY, THE CRAFTSMAN
41 West 34th Street, New York City

CRAFTSMAN FURNITURE

This furniture is a practical expression of the Craftsman idea of simplicity, honesty and beauty as applied to home furnishings. In workmanlike construction, finish, service and comfort, Craftsman furniture, though continually imitated, has never been equalled. Write for our new catalogue.

Of the same general excellence as Craftsman furniture are our rugs, curtains, portières, metal work and other furnishings. We have a new and complete catalogue of these goods, which will be sent if you are interested.

Orders promptly filled through our Mail Order Department. Samples furnished and color schemes suggested. Write to a Craftsman Store.

GUSTAV STICKLEY
THE CRAFTSMAN

| 29 West 34th St., | 1512 H. St., N. W., | 468 Boylston St., |
| New York City | Washington, D. C. | Boston, Mass. |

The Craftsman Workshops, Eastwood, N. Y.